CRITICAL ESSAYS ON

KING LEAR

William Shakespeare

Editors:
Linda Cookson
Bryan Loughrey

Longman Literature Guides

Editors: Linda Cookson and Bryan Loughrey

Titles in the series:

CONTENTS

PREFACE

Like all professional groups, literary critics have developed their own specialised language. This is not necessarily a bad thing. Sometimes complex concepts can only be described in a terminology far removed from everyday speech. Academic jargon, however, creates an unnecessary barrier between the critic and the intelligent but less practised reader.

This danger is particularly acute where scholarly books and articles are re-packaged for a student audience. Critical anthologies, for example, often contain extracts from longer studies originally written for specialists. Deprived of their original context, these passages can puzzle and at times mislead. The essays in this volume, however, are all specially commissioned, self-contained works, written with the needs of students firmly in mind.

This is not to say that the contributors — all experienced critics and teachers — have in any way attempted to simplify the complexity of the issues with which they deal. On the contrary, they explore the central problems of the text from a variety of critical perspectives, reaching conclusions which are challenging and at times mutually contradictory.

They try, however, to present their arguments in a direct, accessible language and to work within the limitations of scope and length which students inevitably face. For this reason, essays are generally rather briefer than is the practice; they address quite specific topics; and, in line with examination requirements, they incorporate precise textual detail into the body of the discussion.

They offer, therefore, working examples of the kind of essay-writing skills which students themselves are expected to develop. Their diversity, however, should act as a reminder that in the field of literary studies there is no such thing as a 'model' answer. Good essays are the outcome of a creative engagement with literature, of sensitive, attentive reading and careful thought. We hope that those contained in this volume will encourage students to return to the most important starting point of all, the text itself, with renewed excitement and the determination to explore more fully their own critical responses.

How to use this volume

Obviously enough, you should start by reading the text in question. The one assumption that all the contributors make is that you are already familiar with this. It would be helpful, of course, to have read further — perhaps other works by the same author or by influential contemporaries. But we don't assume that you have yet had the opportunity to do this and any references to historical background or to other works of literature are explained.

You should, perhaps, have a few things to hand. It is always a good idea to keep a copy of the text nearby when reading critical studies. You will almost certainly want to consult it when checking the context of quotations or pausing to consider the validity of the critic's interpretation. You should also try to have access to a good dictionary, and ideally a copy of a dictionary of literary terms as well. The contributors have tried to avoid jargon and to express themselves clearly and directly. But inevitably there will be occasional words or phrases with which you are unfamiliar. Finally, we would encourage you to make notes, summarising not just the argument of each essay but also your own responses to what you have read. So keep a pencil and notebook at the ready.

Suitably equipped, the best thing to do is simply begin with whichever topic most interests you. We have deliberately organised each volume so that the essays may be read in any order. One consequence of this is that, for the sake of clarity and self-containment, there is occasionally a degree of overlap between essays. But at least you are not forced to follow one — fairly arbitrary — reading sequence.

Each essay is followed by brief 'Afterthoughts', designed to highlight points of critical interest. But remember, these are only there to remind you that it is *your* responsibility to question what you read. The essays printed here are not a series of 'model' answers to be slavishly imitated and in no way should they be regarded as anything other than a guide or stimulus for your own thinking. We hope for a critically involved response: 'That was interesting. But if *I* were tackling the topic . . .!'

Read the essays in this spirit and you'll pick up many of the skills of critical composition in the process. We have, however, tried to provide more explicit advice in 'A practical guide to essay writing'. You may find this helpful, but do not imagine it offers any magic formulas. The quality of your essays ultimately depends on the quality of your engagement with literary texts. We hope this volume spurs you on to read these with greater understanding and to explore your responses in greater depth.

THE TEXTS OF
KING LEAR

Two distinct versions of the play exist. The first, *The History of King Lear*, was published in a quarto (a term which, like folio, refers to the size of paper used by the printer) of 1608. The second, *The Tragedy of King Lear*, was included within the 1623 Folio edition of Shakespeare's plays. This later version is considerably shorter — the mock trial of Lear's daughters is one of several substantial cuts — and contains a number of significant alterations.

Most modern editions are based on a conflation of the two versions. The assumption behind this procedure is that each version imperfectly represents an 'ideal' single play. The texts of plays were often treated in a cavalier fashion by printers and there is no evidence that Shakespeare was concerned to oversee the publication of his works. It is possible, then, that the best way to recover the play as he originally conceived it is to combine elements of both *The History of King Lear* and *The Tragedy of King Lear*.

The editors of the recent Oxford Shakespeare, however, argue that Shakespeare himself was responsible for the revisions and alterations to the texts, probably adapting the play in the light of experience gained from staging the original version. They believe, moreover, that the two versions differ so markedly, both in structure and content, that they must be regarded as separate plays. These views are controversial, but are accepted by many scholars. Three of the essays in this volume, those by Moseley, Gurr and Saunders, take account of the variations to be found in the texts of *King Lear*.

Unless otherwise stated, references in this volume are to the new Arden edition of *King Lear*, but students are advised to consult the Oxford Shakespeare, edited by Stanley Wells and Gary Taylor, where the texts of both versions may be compared.

Cedric Watts

*Cedric Watts is Professor of English at
Sussex University, and author of
numerous scholarly publications.*

ESSAY

Main plot, sub-plot and paradox in *King Lear*

The first time I read *King Lear*, I found it so bewildering and
confusing, so noisy and jarring and (often) so crazy — that if
you'd asked me then to distinguish between the main plot and
the sub-plot, I'd have hesitated before attempting an answer.
Since then, I've given it plenty of re-readings, and the result is
that I now hesitate even longer. There are two reasons for this.

The first reason is that Shakespeare has very cleverly
entangled the apparent main plot and the apparent sub-plot.
Admittedly, in a brief summary the distinction seems clear
enough. There's the plot involving King Lear and his division
of the kingdom: he blesses the wicked daughters, Regan and
Goneril, and curses Cordelia, the virtuous daughter; tardily
learns, through suffering, his mistake; and eventually is poignantly reconciled to Cordelia. Then there's the sub-plot involving
Gloucester and his two sons: he's fooled into favouring Edmund,
the bad son, and spurning Edgar, the good son; tardily learns,
through suffering, his mistake; and eventually is poignantly
reconciled to Edgar. (You'll notice that already there is dupli-
cated phrasing in the summary.) The two plots become progress-
ively entangled. Gloucester is brutally blinded by Cornwall,
husband of Regan; Goneril and Regan, though married, are both

sexually attracted to Edmund, Gloucester's illegitimate son; and their jealous rivalry for his favours leads to their downfall. Goneril poisons Regan and kills herself, after an intercepted letter persuades Albany to order her arrest; rather tardily, Albany becomes an ally of the defeated Lear and Cordelia; Edmund is slain in a duel with Edgar; and Edgar's report that Gloucester had died "twixt two extremes of passion, joy and grief', is soon followed by the death of Lear, which itself seems to express those two 'extremes of passion'.

The second reason is that this intermingling of characters seems simply a consequence of Shakespeare's determination to organise the drama on very strong thematic lines. The more you consider the text thematically, the more you see that the stories of Lear and Gloucester are both subordinate to the same large patterns. In both cases we see the same principles at work: Lear breaches the morality of the family and the laws of statecraft; the consequent suffering deranges him, but during his derange-ment he has moments of moral lucidity, and eventually, contrite, he is reconciled to the daughter who has striven on his behalf. Gloucester, too, has breached the morality of the family (by fathering Edmund during 'good sport' outside wedlock); during the consequent suffering he is blinded, but has moments of insight ('I stumbled when I saw', he says (IV.i.19), and eventu-ally, contrite, he is reconciled to the son who has striven on his behalf. In both cases one of the key terms is the word 'nature'.

Shakespeare emphasises that nature has two contrasting aspects. On the one hand, there is benign or 'green' nature: the creative process at large when it appears to be cooperative with decent humanity. That's the nature of spring-time and summer, of pastoral agriculture, of seed-time and harvest. On the other hand, there is malign or 'red' nature: 'Nature, red in tooth and claw' (in Tennyson's phrase): violent and predatory — we may think of wintry storms and tempests, of ferocious wolves and tigers. Shakespeare sees corresponding forces in *human* nature. Some people are benign, loving, cooperative, nurturing. Other people are malign, vengeful, competitive, rapacious; 'appetitive', in the sense that they may be greedy for power or for illicit sexual pleasure. Edmund says, 'Thou, Nature, art my goddess; to thy law/ My services are bound' (I.ii.1–2). That's partly his way of saying 'If I'm a "natural" child (being illegitimate), I may as well make my liability into an asset by serving nature rather than man-made convention, and seeking power regardless of morality'. The particular 'nature' that he's choosing to serve is the 'appetitive' kind, red in tooth and claw; so he'll be led into alliance with Regan and Goneril, who are associated by the play's imagery with wolves, bears, tigers. So, by a simple paradox, those who serve this malign nature can be seen as 'unnatural', in the sense that they thereby deny benign nature and the traditional loving, affectionate aspects of human nature. You could say that *King Lear* is a battleground in which those two contrasting visions of nature fight to the death.

So both 'main plot' and 'sub-plot' can be seen as expressions of one great cluster of themes identifiable by key terms. There's nature in its benign and malign aspects. There's 'nature versus custom': the essential versus the artificial or man-made. There's the theme of 'blindness (physical or spiritual) and insight', linked to the theme of 'madness and lucidity': both part of the larger theme of 'wisdom gained by suffering'. And a very important theme could be called 'the problem of theodicy'.

'Theodicy' means 'divine justice'. The problem of theodicy is that of reconciling belief in divine justice with the evidence of moral injustice here on earth. It's an ancient and continuing problem for religious believers, and it's the central problem in literary texts classed as tragedies. If there exists a just God (or just gods), why does such divine power permit the existence of apparent injustice all around us? Why is it that good people often suffer, while bad people often prosper? *King Lear* seems determined to express this problem in particularly vivid, searching and harsh ways. Repeatedly in the play, characters invoke or refer to a variety of deities and metaphysical forces: God, Jove, Hecate, Apollo, 'Nature', 'the gods', 'the heavens'; repeatedly there's a questioning of the forces that seem to govern our lives (are they kind, blind or cruel?); and also, insistently, the play seems to hurl at us the sheer raw bloody stuff of human injustice and suffering. The suffering of Lear is painful enough; but the blinding of Gloucester is notoriously horrifying (in the theatre, it still makes audiences flinch and look away); and the death of the virtuous Cordelia seems to set the problem of theodicy in the most explicit of ways. Lear, referring to Cordelia as his 'poor fool' (which editors usually regard as a term of endearment), cries out in his misery:

> And my poor fool is hang'd! No, no, no life!
> Why should a dog, a horse, a rat, have life,
> And thou no breath at all?

(V.iii.304–306)

It's a crucial question in the play, and it's one which commentators often try to answer. As is customary among commentators on Shakespeare, they produce some remarkably conflicting views. Some see the play as pessimistic and sceptical about divine justice: Samuel Johnson, the greatest critic in the eighteenth century, said that he found the death of Cordelia so painful that he could scarcely bring himself to read again the ending of the play until his editorial duties obliged him to do so; he contemplated sadly this text in which 'the wicked prosper, and the virtuous miscarry'. Other critics have seen the play as an affirmation of Christianity. G I Duthie, for example, in his introduction to the 1960 Cambridge text of *King Lear*, says:

> God overthrows the absolutely evil — he destroys the Cornwalls, the Gonerils, the Regans: he is just. God chastens those who err but who can be regenerated — the Lears, the Gloucesters — and in mercy he redeems them: he is just, and merciful. But again, God moves in a mysterious way — he deals strangely with the Cordelias of this world. His methods are inscrutable. Shakespeare presents the whole picture. . . . This, however, can mean 'pessimistic' drama only to those who cannot agree that the play is a Christian play.

When the commentators disagree, one way of trying to clarify our sense of Shakespeare's intentions and meanings is to look at his use of the source-materials. Changes to a source should be a guide to his purposes. If we look at the ways in which he adapted the source-materials of *King Lear*, a very big paradox emerges. It can be summed up by saying that his adaptations seem designed both to strengthen and to weaken the sense of divine ordinance of the events.

First, let's consider the material about Gloucester and his two sons. This derives from the story of the King of Paphlagonia in Sir Philip Sidney's novel, *Arcadia*. The King (like Gloucester) has two sons, one legitimate and one illegitimate; he is tricked by the illegitimate son, Plexirtus, into disowning the legitimate son, Leonatus. Subsequently Plexirtus blinds his aged father and casts him out; Leonatus serves as his guide in the wilderness, deflecting the old man from suicide, and with friends defeats Plexirtus and his men. The King dies after being fully reconciled to Leonatus, who inherits the throne. Evidently, this material is the source of the Gloucester sub-plot of *King Lear*; and though there were various versions of the King Lear story before Shakespeare wrote his play, Shakespeare (scholars believe) was the first writer to combine the Lear material with the Paphlagonia material. And, as we have seen, there are many parallels between the two concurrent stories of misguided parenthood, rivalry between siblings, suffering in the wilderness, and eventual reconciliation of father with loving child. In Shakespeare's play, Lear and Gloucester, during their separate wanderings, gain remarkably similar moral insights. Thus, in Act III, scene iv, lines 28–36, Lear says:

> Poor naked wretches, whereso'er you are,
> That bide the pelting of this pitiless storm,
> How shall your houseless heads and unfed sides,
> Your loop'd and window'd raggedness, defend you
> From seasons such as these? O! I have ta'en
> Too little care of this! Take physic, Pomp;
> Expose thyself to feel what wretches feel,
> That thou mayst shake the superflux to them,
> And show the Heavens more just.

And in Act IV, scene i, lines 63–70, Gloucester says to 'Poor Tom':

> Here, take this purse, thou whom the heav'ns' plagues
> Have humbled to all strokes: that I am wretched
> Makes thee the happier: Heavens, deal so still!
> Let the superfluous and lust-dieted man,
> That slaves your ordinance, that will not see
> Because he does not feel, feel your power quickly;
> So distribution should undo excess,
> And each man have enough.

The similarities in insight are obvious: in both cases, there is a recognition of the need for the high to have compassion and charity for the needs of the low. So when we consider that both Gloucester and Lear have erred, have misjudged their children, have suffered terribly as a consequence, but have come (independently) to kindred wisdom, this clearly creates the impression that their suffering is an *ordained* suffering. We gain the impression that divine powers have acted to punish but also to enlighten these erring noblemen. A repeated pattern implies a pattern-maker. Without the parallelism between the progresses of the two men, which has been created by Shakespeare's combination of the traditional Lear material with Sidney's 'Paphlagonian' material, we would not gain such a strong sense of a divine power at work.

But that's only the first half of the big paradox. The other half, which completes it, is this. If we look at Shakespeare's other changes to that traditional Lear material, we find that his intentions now seem to be quite different. The story of King Lear (or Leir) had been told by various writers before Shakespeare: among others, by Geoffrey of Monmouth, by Higgins in his *Mirror for Magistrates*, by Holinshed in his *Chronicles*, by Spenser in *The Faerie Queene*, and by the author of the anonymous play entitled *The True Chronicle History of King Leir*. And in all these versions, the story of the King ends relatively happily. After his reconcilation to his virtuous daughter, he is restored to the throne, and seems set to live happily ever after. In most versions, he continues to reign until eventually he dies naturally and peacefully of old age. Certainly, in some versions, the daughter then dies by suicide in prison after having been defeated in a rebellion by her nephews; but that happens a very long time after the reconciliation. Only in Shakespeare's text does Cordelia die before Lear; only in Shakespeare's version do we have that hideous sense of reconciliation blighted by the sudden and cruel murder of the daughter; only in Shakespeare's version does the King have happiness so abruptly snatched from his grasp, and receive the mortal shock of seeing the beloved child die. There was no precedent for the utterly harsh and bleak quality of Shakespeare's ending to the story. And you'll notice that Shakespeare has gone out of his way to accentuate that harshness. The death of Cordelia is a consequence, among other things, of sheer absentmindedness: when Kent asks Albany (at V.iii.235–236) where the King is, Albany replies:

> Great thing of us forgot!
> Speak, Edmund, where's the King? and where's Cordelia?

It's fatal forgetfulness: rescue is sent too late. Albany even appeals for divine aid:

> The Gods defend her!

But within half a line, as if in sardonic comment on his appeal to the heavens, Lear enters with Cordelia dead in his arms. Later, Albany tries to reassert a pattern of moral justice:

> All friends shall taste
> The wages of their virtue, and all foes
> The cup of their deservings.
>
> (V.iii.301–303)

And again, the text harshly undercuts this assertion, for it's then that Lear cries 'And my poor fool is hang'd' — as if to say, 'How can this death possibly fit *any* pattern of moral justice?' So, there's the paradox: while some of Shakespeare's changes to the sources seem designed to establish the sense of divine ordinance, others seem designed to challenge any belief in divine ordinance. The stronger our sense of the patterning of the previous events, the stronger will be our sense of the disruption of that patterning at the close. Tragedies usually end sombrely; but the ending of *King Lear* seems to be exceptionally bleak and harsh.

The difference between a paradox and a contradiction is that though a paradox initially poses as a contradiction ('The child is father of the man') it contains its own resolution — on reflection, you can see how it makes sense. By referring to the 'paradox' rather than the 'contradiction' of *King Lear*, I've implied a resolution. And what is it? The answer is in Shakespeare's play *Troilus and Cressida*. There, in Act I, scene iii, Ulysses makes a speech on order. He says that there's a pre-ordained order extending throughout the entire cosmos; everything has its rightful place; but if people cease to respect it and become selfish creatures of appetite, then the whole order collapses:

And appetite, an universal wolf,
So doubly seconded with will and power,
Must make perforce an universal prey,
And last eat up himself.

If people deny the established order, then chaos and destruction ensue: and he does not say that the divine powers are able to restore order. He appears to be saying, 'A God whom we deny — is a God who then may die'. That God may strike back for a while, punishing those who disrupted the order; but in the general collapse, he too may perish or depart. I think that that is the idea or nightmare that Shakespeare dramatised in *King Lear*. But I may be wrong. *King Lear* is a wild, violent, poignant and volcanic text; sometimes simple, sometimes obscure and complex; it voices sanity and madness, evil and love, chaos and order. The play is a mixture of folk tale, fantasy, parable and grim realism. Its potential is greater than any prosaic commentator can express or summarise. Read it, see it, and judge for yourself.

AFTERTHOUGHTS

1

What contrasting aspects of 'nature' does Watts identify (pages 12–13)? Compare his analysis with Smith's arguments on pages 35–37.

2

What conclusions does Watts draw from his analysis of Shakespeare's 'use of source materials' (pages 14–17)?

3

Compare Watts's views on 'theodicy' with Cheetham's essay on pages 55–63.

4

What relationship is established in this essay between 'paradox' and 'double plot'?

John Cunningham

*John Cunningham was until recently
Head of English at Varndean Sixth
Form College. He is the author of
numerous critical studies.*

ESSAY

King Lear:
the opening scenes

Readers or spectators coming to *King Lear* for the first time are often seriously prejudiced against the play by the content of the first two scenes. It is not uncommon to hear comments on the 'incredible stupidity' of Lear in choosing a daughter, whose only fault is honesty, as the object of hatred and rejection, while he accepts the glib praises of her elders, who are manifestly false; there is a similar response to Gloucester for being so ready to believe the suggestions of a son who is so obviously self-interested. Those who can overcome what they feel is an outrage to their own common sense may go on to experience the rest of the play as one of Shakespeare's greatest triumphs, but there remains an uncomfortable suspicion that he wrote a bad first Act in order to write four good ones. There is no lack of critical theory to explain — or explain away — this paradox. Some of these theories we shall explore in an attempt to arrive at our own.

The simplest view is that Shakespeare made a mess of it; and it is right that we remind ourselves of a truth — he did not always write well or even carefully: but this play is so immense and powerful that it is hard to suppose he did not take care over the opening. He had, after all, to catch and hold the attention of an audience a good deal more rumbustious than most modern ones.

A more sophisticated version of this theory is that he was obliged to set up his plot in a rather arbitrary way in order to build his play upon it. Similar theories are advanced in explanation of plots and characters in other plays: for instance, in *Othello* it is said that Iago has insufficient motive for his implacable pursuit of the hero, so critics suggest that he must be an obligatory villain like the wicked witch in a child's story. The early comedies often depend upon a situation wholly improbable, while in *The Tempest*, his last work, characters are drawn together in a quite unbelievable way for the purposes of the action. Yet, though that play has its sombre elements, it is nevertheless a comedy and we may feel that tragedy should rise above such artifices. Lear's is not the story of the Three Little Pigs whose motives for building their houses we never question, since all that matters to the story is that they did so.

This mention of the childish tale of the Three Little Pigs — which, as such folk stories often are, may be very old indeed — brings me to an even more scholarly line of approach. This tells us that we may consider the first part of *Lear* as a myth, an archetypal story of a daughter wrongly undervalued (like Cinderella) and of evil scheming successfully until it brings its own punishment — in the original version Cinderella's sisters were blinded. There has been much exploration of the origins of the play, and many learned notes have been written about a Celtic sea-god whose name variously spelt is like that of the king. Such theories can be quite fascinating to pursue but are of no help at all on the stage — the actors cannot readily suggest that they are acting in a different way for the first half an hour — and it is only on the stage that Shakespeare's plays 'exist': they were written not to be printed or published, still less to be studied, but to remain the precious property of the playhouse.

Starting from this viewpoint, we may begin our own evaluation of the theatrical validity of our theory by looking at the strength of the case for asserting a lack of consistency between the first and remaining Acts. At least one view in the present century has asserted that inconsistency is of no significance at all: that, in the rapid movement of an Elizabethan production, the 'two-hours' traffic of our stage' as it is called in *Romeo and Juliet*, no one was really aware of changes of behaviour in the characters except in the most general way. So Lear and Gloucester are impetuous and imperious fathers at the beginning who gradually learn sense.

Yet the words 'impetuous and imperious' seem too kind. Both men reject their children with quite extraordinary violence. After two brief questions — 'goes thy heart with this? . . . So young, and so untender?' — Lear launches into a ferocious diatribe against his favourite daughter. Calling upon the mightiest forces of nature — 'the sacred radiance of the sun,/ the mysteries of Hecate and the night' — he rejects her for ever. This rejection is reinforced with an extravagant and disgusting image:

> The barbarous Scythian
> Or he that makes his generation messes
> To gorge his appetite

(I.i.115–117)

will, says Lear, be as welcome to him as his 'sometime daughter'. When Kent tries to defend her, he turns on him, an old and trusted courtier, with equal ferocity and banishes him. When Burgundy appears to claim his bride, Lear speaks of her as if he were in the slave-market and she upon the block to be bid for:

> Sir, there she stands:
> If aught within that little-seeming substance
> . . . may fitly like your Grace,
> She's there, and she is yours.

(I.i.196–200)

Burgundy's refusal to take her without a dowry, a refusal which would have seemed good sense, not poor chivalry, when the play was written, adds to her very public humiliation and rouses both love and compassion in France, whose speech rather emphasises the wrong judgement of others than praises his own. Lear's last act of contempt towards the girl is to leave the stage with the man who has just declined her — 'Come, noble Burgundy' — and abandon her to her stranger-husband and the unkind comments of her sisters. We ask ourselves if this can be the man who, in the final Act, when the future for father and daughter is hopeless, comforts her as he would a child:

> Come, lets away to prison;
> We two alone will sing like birds in the cage
>   . . . and so we'll live,
> And pray and sing, and tell old tales, and laugh
> At gilded butterflies, and hear poor rogues
> Talk of court news . . .

(V.iii.8–14)

Surely it is hard to see consistency here?

So with Gloucester. At the end of the play his behaviour could hardly be less impressive. He comes onto the stage in the second scene tut-tutting about what the world is coming to nowadays like every caricaturist's picture of a fuddy-duddy; some crude business with a carefully concealed revealed letter, a pretended reluctance to speak ill of the absent, and he is convinced that his son plots against his life, and sets an agent to spy on him with full powers to act as he sees fit. The scene presents real difficulties to modern actors, for Gloucester seems so silly and Edmund so smart that there is often laughter at the deception.

The difficulty for us, then, is to try to reconcile these apparent absurdities in a way that makes sense to the student and can be performed by the actor.

We are given a possible clue to Shakespeare's intentions in Regan's remark at the end of the first scene that Lear 'hath ever but slenderly known himself'. If we refer to the beginning of that scene, to Lear's first entrance in fact, we at once see signs of what she is talking about. He enters his court, gives no sort of greeting or acknowledgement to the courtiers, snaps out an order to the oldest man present to 'attend the lords of France and Burgundy', and follows this imperious beginning by an extraordinary show of secretiveness and demand. He speaks of his 'darker purpose', an image which is scarcely accidental in a play whose major metaphor is blindness (as we shall perceive) and proceeds to tell the court he will have his cake and eat it: he will 'shake off all cares and business' but he will also retain 'the name and the addition to a king' while the 'execution', that is the responsibilities, must be shared by his sons-in-law. He wants power without responsibilities. On a more domestic level, he proposes to stay, by monthly rotation, in the homes of each of his daughters in turn — and with a large train of followers: an excellent recipe for friction.

Our first impressions, then, are of a man jealous of his power and rank, imperious in manner, highly demanding. He demands something else which none of us may command: love. So greedy is he for the expression of love in its outward form that he makes it a condition of the division of his kingdom:

> Which of you shall we say doth love us most?
> That we our largest bounty may extend
> Where nature doth with merit challenge.
>
> (I.i.50–52)

This association of 'nature', that is family affection, with merit is confused but not unfamiliar. It is an unhappy aspect of the old that they will sometimes demand affection on the grounds that it will be rewarded later — in the will: Lear is activating his will before he is dead, as the Fool later tells him.

So greedy is he for a display of fondness that the slightest suggestion that he is not loved above all else meets with instant fury out of all proportion to the imagined slight. Cordelia tells him honestly that she loves him as a daughter but, being a woman, she will one day have a duty, as her sisters already have, to love a husband more. Shakespeare seems to have a strong sympathy for the ambivalent position which daughters might so find themselves in, and uses this situation to good effect elsewhere: Shylock's Jessica is torn apart in this way, and so is Othello's wife, who faces her father on the same issue in public — and reminds him that his wife once had to make the choice she now does.

Her father refuses to listen, and so does Lear. Anything contrary to his notion of what is owing to him is intolerable — he exiles the faithful Kent for speaking in Cordelia's defence — and so the scene sweeps to its conclusion, daughter and courtier alike banished for ever.

Again we feel that this is childish. We are all familiar with the phrase 'second childhood' and that is how the older daughters seem to see his behaviour: 'You see how full of changes his age is,' says Goneril. Yet it is possible to argue, and to translate that argument into stage performance, that Lear is wholly consistent throughout this scene — and what follows.

We have noticed that he must always be the centre of attention, that all his commands, some of them utterly unrealistic, must be obeyed, that any supposed opposition to his will meets with violent rejection, that he needs to be constantly reassured that he is loved and respected, that his power is still absolute — though he does not want to bear any of the responsibility of that power. While there are dangers in applying the terms of modern psychology too glibly to the work of a writer who probably did not think of 'character' quite as we do, it can be argued that we have here a classic, text-book case of a distressing condition well known in the elderly: senile dementia. The phrase sounds unkind, but the state can perhaps be seen as the desperate effort of the subconscious to assert that we are not really old or mortal, that we still command love and respect, that we have not lost our power. So understood, it is a condition to be pitied; but when it develops in someone who has a great deal of real power it can be highly dangerous — our own century is not lacking in some disquieting studies of the amount of power held by elderly heads of state — and another monarch, Claudius in *Hamlet*, says 'Madness in great ones must not unwatched go'. Lear is still entitled to exercise absolute power over his subjects and such a condition in him is of concern to the whole country, not just his family.

Gloucester seems, on the other hand, to endanger only those who are near to him: if we are to pursue the 'clinical' approach we have attempted for Lear, how is he to be 'diagnosed'?

As with his king, Gloucester's opening passage in the play is highly suggestive, and in more than one sense: he and Kent open the play itself in some casual, low-key chat, which Shakespeare gives in prose, not verse, to emphasise its ordinariness. What is its tone? After a brief mention of who is the likely favourite in the inheritance stakes, the two men fall to some rather sniggering, man-of-the-world exchanges about Gloucester's bastard son — who is listening to them without expressing any feelings on the matter. The elderly noble indulges in sexual reminiscence: 'this knave came something saucily to the world before he was sent for, yet was his mother fair; there was good sport at his making (I.i.20–22). As Edgar is the older, it appears that this was an adulterous union, for good measure. This kind of talk is always somewhat offensive in its boasting overtones and perhaps more so among the old as here: is this not Lear's disease in a less marked form? For most men their virility is a symbol of power and youthful energy, and to refer to the fiery exploits of their earlier years is a means to deny or defy age itself. This, like Cordelia's dilemma, Shakespeare also understood well: he makes Polonius speak in an unpleasantly knowing way about what he once 'suffered for love' and take vicarious delight in spying upon his own son's misbehaviour as a reflection of his father; while similar obsessions with waning powers appear in *Othello*.

Gloucester's son, like Polonius's, is a symbol of his own youth. His legitimate son is a reminder of domesticity — Edmund puts it sharply when he says such children are begotten 'within a dull, stale, tired bed . . ./ Got 'tween asleep and wake'. When Gloucester encounters Edmund, his mind full of the upheavals of the first scene, he is readily receptive to the notion that his child, like Cordelia, does not love him, especially when he is told so by the favoured product of his youthful amours. He, too, feels the need for love and the anxiety to assert his authority as still effective; and Lear's behaviour has promoted in him a deep sense of doubt — 'I would unstate myself to be in due resolution' (I.ii.96–97) — and a feeling that the world as he thinks he knows it is upside down. The two fathers complement one another — not in stupidity, but in the reasons for their 'stupid' acts. In the light of some of the known manifestations of ageing, they make sense.

If we are to try to interpret the two fathers in terms of modern psychology, we may need to go back to Shakespeare's own day to understand the behaviour of the children. It is common knowledge that the position of women was then very different from what obtains nowadays. A man's daughters were, in a real sense, his property to dispose of until they married: to marry well they had to have a dowry; when married they, and their possessions, became the sole property of their husbands. Above all, women were to obey men. That is the heart of a play which offends many modern readers, *The Taming of the Shrew*: for Katherine to bully her husband is not just bad luck for him but is striking at the whole order of society as then conceived.

The same perversion of the supposed pattern of things is strikingly shown by Goneril, who for too long controls her husband, and by both daughters in ultimately treating their father as a troublesome child; it is reflected horribly, too, in Regan's torturing of old Gloucester. Cordelia, having no status except as a daughter, dares much in crossing her father at all, but pleads the higher cause of truthfulness — and a later duty to a husband. As the play develops, she reveals herself as the truest of daughters, carrying out her 'natural' duty of protecting and sheltering Lear, and doing that duty with what does not always accompany it, love.

If women were at a natural disadvantage in this world, so too were 'natural' sons. Bastards could not inherit — as was the case until very recently in English law — unless some special dispensation was made for them. Gloucester may seem to take his responsibilities towards the youth he says he likes rather lightly: 'He hath been out nine years, and away he shall again'. A bastard had to make his own way in a hard world, and Edmund may well ask the gods to 'stand up' for him and his kind. His arguments are dishonest and self-seeking but they are to some extent based on necessity and would have been understood, if not sympathised with, at the time of the play's composition.

We may, then, amass evidence and theory to suggest that the first two scenes of the play make sense, but audience reaction still tends to be that these men are 'stupid' in so signally failing to see what is obvious to everyone else, including the other characters. Stupidity is a special form of blindness, a refusal to see. Earlier we have suggested that blindness is a 'major metaphor' in the play, and it is now possible to see how that metaphor is introduced in the very scenes we have been studying. After Lear's reference to his 'darker purpose', we hear Goneril speak for the first time: her opening words are:

> Sir, I love you more than word can wield the matter,
> Dearer than eyesight, space and liberty

(I.i.54–55)

And her sister is soon talking of 'the most precious square of sense', which surely includes the sense of vision, precious indeed. Cursing his youngest, Lear invokes 'The mysteries of

Hecate and the night', and charges Kent to 'avoid my sight', soon repeating this — 'Out of my sight!' — to which Kent replies:

> See better, Lear, and let me still remain
> The true blank of thine eye.

(I.i.154–158)

Cordelia assures France that she is guilty of no moral taint but lacks a 'still-soliciting eye'. However, Lear is adamant that she must go:

>   . . . for we
> Have no such daughter, nor shall ever see
> That face of hers again . . .

(I.i.262–264)

Saying her farewells to her sisters, Cordelia leaves them:

> The jewels of our father, with wash'd eyes

(I.i.267)

This theme, of sight and darkness, so marked in frequency in the first scene, is picked up in the second. 'Come; if it be nothing, I shall not need spectacles,' says Gloucester demanding to see the letter, and he goes on to talk of the 'eclipses' that portend no good. When Edmund has dealt with him and with the bewildered Edgar, he is left on stage to tell us, in the concluding lines of the two scenes we are considering:

> My practices ride easy. I see the business.

It is beyond the scope of this essay to pursue the matter further, but it is a well-known analysis of the play that Lear does not sanely see until he is mad and Gloucester does not see the truth until he is literally blind. The basis of this paradox is, as we have seen, most carefully prepared in the opening so often rejected as clumsy. If these men are stupid, their presentation is not.

We end by asking what wisdom they learn in what follows. In the case of Gloucester this is easy: he learns acceptance, expressed in one of the play's most famous lines, 'Ripeness is all' (Edgar, V.ii.11). He learns it through love, the love of his true son, far removed from the 'good sport' of his false son's begetting.

Lear, as we have earlier suggested, shocked out of his mania by a violent reversal of his role, learns how to be a true father, and touchingly comforts the once despised Cordelia when they are sent to prison, just as he later regains his doubted strength and kills the man who hangs her: but he meets greater trials than that, having to face a question which gives the play an extraordinary power and universality. We are all aware, never more so than today, that in our world the good and the innocent often suffer cruelly and without any apparent cause. In *King Lear* there is no comforting notion of another world where we may hope for recompense for the injustice of this. Lear asks the eternal question — Why *me*? Why *her*?:

> Why should a dog, a horse, a rat have life
> And thou no breath at all?

But as, with his 'dull sight', he peers into the obscure pain of human destiny, no answer is vouchsafed. His last words are 'Look there,' but there is nothing to see, even if the final lines of the play assure us that we 'shall never see so much'. What did the 'incredibly stupid' man perceive? Though some critics have claimed he dies happy, believing that he sees living movement in Cordelia, this is to deny the whole force of the play. He sees, perhaps, that we cannot hope to grasp the meaning of our destiny and that we must abide as best we may the consequences of our actions: the folly of these two men, for whatever reason, in the opening Act brings frightful sufferings upon them both; but, worse still, it involves those who are wholly blameless. There is a truth here that is greater than the need for the 'realism' that may be important in documentaries but is wholly subsidiary in works of art.

AFTERTHOUGHTS

1

Did *you* find any problems in accepting the first two scenes of *King Lear*?

2

Do you agree that theories of the sort Cunningham describes in paragraph four are 'of no help at all on the stage' (page 21)?

3

How appropriate is it to adopt a 'clinical approach' (page 25) towards character study?

4

Does Cunningham convince you that the theme of seeing and blindness is established in the first two scenes of the play?

Nigel Smith

*Nigel Smith is Lecturer in English at
Keble College, Oxford.*

ESSAY

Forms of kingship in
King Lear

> No blown ambition doth our arms incite,
> But love, dear love, and our ag'd father's right.
>
> (*King Lear*, IV. iv. 27–28)

Renaissance drama, especially tragedy, placed rulers at the
centre of the stage. Tragedies of state exposed the psychological
shortcomings which lead to the fall of princes and the terrifying
social consequences which this could have. Whether plays were
performed at court or in the public theatres, they retained the
royal figure as their central concern, and sought to address the
monarch of the day, to compliment and (within limits) to offer
advice. Sir Philip Sidney, the Elizabethan soldier, statesman
and writer, was optimistic concerning the uses of tragedy. For
him, it made 'kings fear to be tyrants, and tyrants manifest
their tyrannical humours', sentiments echoed in Shakespeare's
play by Edgar and Albany.[1]

Along with *Measure for Measure* and *Macbeth*, *King Lear*
was one of the plays written and performed during the first

---

[1] Sir Philip Sidney, *A Defence of Poetry*, edited by J A Van Dorsten (Oxford,
1966), p.45.

years of the reign of King James I. When Queen Elizabeth died, and was succeeded by James (who was already King of Scotland), everyone felt the change. This was because of the large degree of personality in high politics, James's eccentric but inflexible nature being in contrast to Elizabeth's wily diplomacy. Of James, the historian Conrad Russell writes:

> Though James was married, and had children, there was little doubt that he was homosexual by inclination, and though this caused less moral indignation than it might do today, it did create considerable feeling about the grounds on which patronage and preferment might be awarded. He had a poor head for drink, and frequently failed to make sufficient allowance for it. He showed an undignified curiosity on unsuitable occasions.[2]

The nation had to adapt its comprehension of the symbolic value of kingship to the new reality. An heirless queen had been replaced by a king with children, but a king with embarrassing manners, who was lazy, vacillating, and whose speeches were 'verbose, plaintive and pompous' despite his proclaimed interest in the dignity of majesty.[3] Elizabethan literature had striven hard to fit chivalric and martial trappings to a woman. Edmund Spenser's long poem *The Faerie Queene* (1590–1596) is a celebration of the Queen. The history plays of the 1590s, including Shakespeare's, were obsessed with the problem of monarchical succession, and the crises which occurred when successions were interrupted. How much Shakespeare knew about the King is difficult to tell. What is clear is that the new monarch exercised Shakespeare's creative powers in a new way.

We also know that King James watched a performance of the play at Whitehall on 26 December 1606.[4] On the surface, *King Lear* tells King James how not to rule. James, who had united a divided and unruly Scotland, and who ruled over Scot-

---

[2] Conrad Russell, *The Crisis of Parliaments. English History 1509–1660* (Oxford, 1971), p.258.
[3] Ibid., loc. cit.
[4] Introduction to William Shakespeare, *King Lear*, edited by Kenneth Muir (London, 1952), p.xviii.

land and England (he was party to the earliest and unpopular plans to join the two kingdoms), was set beside Lear, who divides his kingdom between two daughters and lives to see the loss of all as a consequence. In the division is a search for nationhood or national identity.

We do not know whether James wanted to see the play for any particular reason, or what Shakespeare's intentions were.[5] What is clear is that — in as much as the play presented a reflection of the eccentric King to himself — the play also incorporated a safeguard against royal wrath because opinions which were similar to those of James's critics were put into the mouths of Lear's oppressors. Thus, although the pomposity of James might have been reflected in Lear's speeches (and the language of the play is full of echoes of speeches, especially from James's famous oration at the opening of Parliament in March, 1604), possible references to James's liberal creation of noble titles, the expense of his household and his frequent lack of interest in affairs of state in favour of hunting are contained within Goneril's and Regan's complaints to Lear about his excessive burdening of the state in maintaining large numbers of knights and hunting. It may be that several passages which appear in the first printed edition of the play were censored; for instance, the Fool's reference to the King's giving away of all his titles, and a mock trial which the mad Lear conducted against his daughters. If this was the case, then parts of the earlier version of the play were considered too close to the royal bone. Yet the play remains ambivalent in its presentation of any line of criticism. King James is ultimately praised while seeing an image of kingship not uncritical of his own person.

It has often been noticed that the historical setting of *King Lear* is contradictory and anachronistic. The Fool speaks his prophecy 'before' Merlin's time, and the language of the play reflects a pagan society, Lear being a British king who reigned

---

[5] For further details and discussion on this issue, see Gary Taylor, 'Monopolies, Show Trials, Disaster, and Invasion: *King Lear* and Censorship', in *The Division of the Kingdoms*, edited by Gary Taylor and Michael Warren (Oxford, 1984), pp.75–117, which is controverted by Annabel Patterson, *Censorship and Interpretation. The Conditions of Writing and Reading in Early Modern England* (Madison, Wisconsin, 1984), pp.60–64, 72.

before the founding of Rome, according to the chronicles. Yet the play is full of references to contemporary history, and to Christian symbolism. For this reason, *King Lear* is usually seen as a 'timeless' play, dealing in 'elemental' truths.

This timelessness is a myth. The language of kingship in the play relates directly to the hot issues in political theory in Shakespeare and King James's day. Lear lets his kingdom go to wrack by letting powerful factions breed and destroy each other, and the wealth of the kingdom along with it. The consequence of abdication in favour of Goneril and Regan is the rise of the 'loyalist' faction of Kent, Gloucester and Cordelia, and a threatened war between Albany and Cornwall. Edmund eventually plots to destroy Cornwall, Albany, Regan and Goneril, whichever course will serve his own aggrandisement, and there are further rumours and hints of plots to murder Lear, Gloucester and Albany.

The tyranny of warring factions which rages in Britain is challenged by a foreign power, Cordelia, as Queen of France. The point would not have been lost on Shakespeare's audience. For the forty years before James's accession, France had been divided by political and civil strife after the untimely death in a joust of Henri II in 1559. His widow, Catherine de Medici, had tried in vain to rule through Henri's two young sons, against rising religious factionalism among powerful aristocratic groups. It took a strong king, Henri IV, to pacify and unite the country in the 1590s.

The great intellectual inheritance of these French 'Wars of Religion' was the body of 'resistance theory', a debate focusing upon the question of when and how a tyrannous monarch may be resisted legitimately or even deposed.[6] The French Protestant nobility argued that if their traditional rights as subjects were threatened by the king, then he could be resisted. Nevertheless, the most influential political thinker in France, Jean Bodin, argued that legitimate resistance to a tyrant could only come through the intervention of another prince.[7]

---

[6] See Quentin Skinner, *The Foundation of Modern Political Thought*, 2 vols. (Cambridge, 1978), 2, pp.189–348.
[7] See Jean Bodin, *Six Books of the Commonwealth*, edited by M J Tooley (Oxford, 1955), pp.66, 69.

Cordelia's invasion may be seen as a form of resistance which would have been consistent with King James's viewpoint. In this sense, *King Lear* finds in the recently developed resistance theory new matter for tragic drama. Indeed, *King Lear* is not a revenge play, like *Hamlet* or *Macbeth*, but a more complex and demanding exploration of political desire and human nature. 'Revenge' is a word used only by the most vicious character in the play, Cornwall, and the word emphasises his tyrannical nature, diminished in human terms but dangerous and brutal. When Gloucester talks of the 'tyrannous night' taking 'hold' of Lear, he is saying by association that Lear is subject to the tyranny of Regan and her husband, Cornwall. *King Lear* exceeds the boundaries of revenge drama by engaging with the terms of a current issue in European politics.

The word 'nature' is highly important here, since resistance theory was based upon a set of ideas called 'natural law'. These were understood to be principles of sociability and human well-being which had arrived 'by nature' after the fall of Adam and Eve, in order to protect humankind from its own corrupt being. The appeal to natural law is one of the foundations of modern ideas of political liberty, though in the Renaissance it was more often a means of objecting to royal authority. So it was used by Catholic thinkers against German Protestant princes in the sixteenth century, and by Parliament against Charles I several decades after Shakespeare lived. A tyrant could be defined and resisted if he was alienating the principles of natural law which described the condition of the subject's well-being. Shakespeare had no opportunity, and no desire, to subvert royal authority in this way, and James in any case accepted to some degree the argument from natural law. Rather, Shakespeare was able to show the different and conflicting ways in which the appeal to 'nature' or natural law could be made. The endless succession of rebellion and displacement in Shakespeare's history plays is replaced in *King Lear* by a sceptical exploration of 'nature' in relation to the abuse of power which reflects the growing personal power of Renaissance monarchs (of whom James I was no exception), over and against the more traditional notion of the king as a judge who should look after the well-being of his people. Lear must learn the meaning of 'true need' (II.iv.268) in his subjects in order to comprehend the irresponsibility of his abdication.

The word 'nature' is used in *King Lear* thirty-seven times, and in a variety of ways, not all of them consistent. Both Lear and Edmund address a goddess Nature, but they mean different things. When Lear divides his kingdom, he regards 'nature' as almost synonymous which rank, descriptive of nobility. He wants to see which of his daughters by 'nature doth with merit challenge' (I.i.52) their claim to the greatest portion, and of Kent's intervention on behalf of Cordelia says, 'nor our nature nor our place can bear' (I.i.170). For Edmund, 'nature' names the set of qualities which exists anterior to the custom of legitimate birthright, and by which he means to gain advancement. Lear's idea of nature he is prepared to ignore in favour of 'loyalty' to Cornwall. The viewpoint expressed by Lear is followed by Gloucester who associates legitimacy as natural with the proper order of the natural world and with property. Deceived by Edmund, he promises 'of my land,/ Loyal and natural boy . . ./ To make thee capable' (II.i.82–84). The action of the play, of course, centres on Lear's relationships with his daughters. In his eyes, they become his property by nature, but it is at this point, where kings should listen to advice from their subjects (and Lear does not) that Lear's version of nature is offended and his world begins to disintegrate. This 'nature' is offended not by Cordelia but by Lear when he does not understand her way of communicating loyalty and love ('nothing will come of nothing' — I.i.89), and tyranny is the result, mostly exercised by the two daughters left in England and by Cornwall.

When subjects, subject to tyranny, lose their rights, they become slaves — which is the point of Kent's disguise as a servant, symbolically presenting himself as a subject devoid of rights by nature, loyally accepted by Lear as a servant, but cruelly treated as a 'slave' and below nature by Cornwall. However much Lear is responsible for his predicament, he regards himself as a rightful king and father whose authority has been usurped at home and in the state. As the quotation at the beginning of this essay makes clear, Cordelia regards her invasion as a defence of her father's 'right'. It is implied that Goneril and Regan have both broken a written contract for the terms of Lear's retirement. 'Nature' is sufficiently offended when Cornwall is mutilating Gloucester that social ranks dissolve and Cornwall is wounded (mortally we learn later) by a servant.

On the heath, Lear realises what he has become. With neither power nor status, he is a 'slave' to the elements. This is a paradox, since as King he should have least fear of this tyranny by nature, the storm. But the only way he can articulate his feelings for his daughters is to imagine himself as the victim of nature, in a primitive state of nature, and at the mercy of divine justice: 'Tremble, thou wretch,/ That hast within thee undivulged crimes,/ Unwhipp'd of Justice' (III.ii.51–53). The storm gives him something external with which to identify his internal frustration, but as Kent says, to endure such exposure is beyond man's nature. In this sense, the heath scene presents a dramatic reversal of the usual explanation for natural laws, which were supposed to arise as a consequence of man's fall, to protect him from the state of nature. If Lear on the heath is elemental man in a state of nature, it is because he has alienated the principles of natural law by his original action. The state of nature is produced by an absence of just and natural relations between prince and subjects, rather than being consequent upon it.

James I's advice to his son, *Basilikon Doron* (1599), was in fact part of a tradition of writing, supposedly stretching back to Aristotle, in which the protective role of the ruler was put forth. There was a marked concern for the health of the King himself: a healthy monarch helped to make a healthy state, and in symbolic terms, the body of the king was seen as synonymous with the body of the state (the body politic). Gradually, this 'advice to princes' literature came to offer more specific advice on matters of statecraft, sometimes referring to particular problems or events in specific reigns.

Lear ruins his health. In the scene on the heath, in his rage at impotence, betrayal and cruelty, he takes off his clothes ('Off, off, you lendings' (III.iv.106–107)), exposing himself to the elements. The storm on the heath has often been seen as a symbolic extension of Lear's rage, and as a natural manifestation of the rupturing of political and domestic orders. The body of the king and the body of the state are simultaneously manifested to the audience in a noisy and harrowing apocalypse.

Lear learns on the heath through a kind of empathy with the dispossessed:

> Poor naked wretches, whereso'er you are,
> That bide the pelting of this pitiless storm,
> How shall your houseless heads and unfed sides,
> Your loop'd and window'd raggedness, defend you
> From seasons such as these? O! I have ta'en
> Too little care of this.

$$\text{(III.iv.28–33)}$$

Through a role-swopping with those at the bottom of the social hierarchy (vagabonds, beggars and madmen), Lear sees something of his selfishness and he is moved towards charity. It is a means of achieving awareness through inversion: the way things should be is perceived most clearly when, as a consequence of the way things *are*, the world is turned upside-down. Here, Shakespeare draws on another Renaissance tradition, that of folly. From the beginning of the play, at the point of division, we see Lear swap places with his Fool, and of this inversion we are constantly reminded. The Fool becomes a repository of wisdom. Lear a 'very foolish fond old man' (IV.vii.60). For his combination of eccentricity and learnedness, James I was known as 'the wisest fool in Christendom'. There is a clear gap between Lear and King James, but was Shakespeare trying to make a broad comparison between the real and the stage kings apparent?

The folly tradition originated in Erasmus's *In Praise of Folly* (1509) and Sir Thomas More's *Utopia*, men being concerned to reveal through folly the abuses of the great and the supposedly wise. Fools were prophets, revealing the dire truth behind false appearances, and through that revelation calling down divine grace in the hope of personal and social renewal. More never intended that the world he portrayed imaginatively (in which there was no property) should be created. Rather, he hoped that the juxtaposition of the grim state of affairs in the Europe of his day with the folly-inspired utopian vision would lead men to live better lives. The 'communism' was not in the presented ideal society but through the ironic vision of looking at the way things are and the way things should be simultaneously. Unfortunately, More was misinterpreted, his utopian vision being taken

at face value for most of the ﹒
however, seems to have understᴄ
the folly tradition by having not
Fool and Edgar disguised as Poor
a distinct lesson).

/King Lear is *dystopian*, the oppo﹒
see how society should become, but hᴠ
abuses. The effect of the division of the
horrifying never-never world in which prᴠ
with them the principles of charity and oᴸ
and politically. The old way of the king w   ˴ jester
(who would be punished if he spoke out of ˏ   ﹒ matters of
state) is displaced by a split vision of folly: ᴏne old impotent
King and wise Fool, together with Poor Tom, who feigns
madness in order to teach his by then blinded father, Gloucester,
the true meaning of trust and filial loyalty. Lear becomes the
'natural fool of Fortune' (IV.vi.189), the phrase aptly combining
the three dominant aspects of the play.

The word 'utopia' means literally 'nowhere', and resonances
of this are carried powerfully within Shakespeare's play.
'Nothing will come of nothing' is prophetic: by dividing the
kingdom, Lear becomes nothing and it becomes nothing but a
barren, stormy, ravaged wasteland. The tragedy is effected by
the failure of redemption: neither Lear nor Cordelia survive. In
a secular imitation of Christopher Marlowe's play, *Dr Faustus*
(1592), as soon as Lear contracts to divide his kingdom, he is
seen to outlive himself, to 'usurp' his life (V.iii.316), not through
tyranny but through folly. Unlike Faustus, it is not a contract
made in part through the agency of the devil, but a decision
entirely his own. In his madness, Lear eventually thinks that
he is dead and mistakes Cordelia for the spirit of another dead
person (IV.vii.49). His death is a confirmation of this awareness,
that we have been 'from [the] first of difference and decay'
(V.iii.287). Over the dead Cordelia, Lear hangs between life and
death, pointing up his unbelief at what his up-ending of the
state has caused with tormented anguish: 'Never, never, never,
never, never' (V.iii.306). A moment later, Lear dies (arguably)
thinking that he sees life on the lips of his dead daughter. As
his folly ends in his death, so he carries with him the illusion
that 'nothing' and 'never' have been forestalled.

is being nothing. Lear is foolish in his act of
Edgar must adopt the guise of a mad fool, Poor
reby also signifying the cruel rejection by his father,
ar I nothing am' (II.iii.21). Just as Lear thinks he is a spirit,
o the Fool and others regard Edgar as a spirit. His own guise
involves the pretence that he is possessed by a multitude of evil
spirits, and his observation on the self-mortifications of the
wandering insane, who 'Strike in their numb'd and mortified
bare arms/ Pins, wooden pricks, nails, sprigs of rosemary'
(II.iii.15–16). It is in this also supernatural realm that Lear
comes to be, as, echoing Edgar's words, he is not sure that
feeling a pin prick is an assurance of mortal status. The message
of charity born by Edgar as Poor Tom is conveyed through baseness: 'To take the basest and most poorest shape/ That ever
penury, in contempt of man,/ Brought near to beast' (II.iii.7–9).
In this Edgar (and ultimately Lear after him) is imitating that
gestural behaviour of biblical kingship, when King David
danced naked like a fool before his wife, Michal (2 Samuel
6: 16–23). True majesty has, according to this tradition, a justification for this behaviour, but it is one which Lear does not
fully understand.

David's revelry actually occasioned a rupture in his
relationship with Michal: he carried on his 'baseness' with the
maidservants and she, despising him, bore him no children.
Such royal behaviour does not result in infertility. According to
the customs of Hebraic kingship, David simply plants his seed
elsewhere. For the ageing Lear, however, the loss of status and
subjection by his daughters makes him invoke in pathetic rage
his own imagined rupturings of the natural order as a punishment: 'Dry up in her [Goneril] the organs of increase,/ And from
her derogate body never spring/ A babe to honour her!'
(I.iv.277–279). Lear is diminished as we become aware of the
futility of his roarings. At the same time, we remember the
selfish behaviour of Lear in the first scene, and Regan's
warning, 'he hath ever but slenderly known himself' (I.i.292–293).
Is there here some distanced portrait of the ill-tempered,
pompous Scottish king, whose own sexuality is transposed in
Lear's hatred of his daughters, and brought to tragic violence
in the gouging out of eyes (eyes being shaped like eggs or
wombs, and suggesting the sexual order of nature)?

Cordelia, who, unlike her father, is able to control her 'rebel-like' passions in grief at Lear's state, is unable to prevent capture and the murderous cruelty of Edmund. Her hanging signals the end of Lear and the grim, lifeless conclusion of the play. There is no redemption: Edgar prophesies a short life for any left remaining. If King James paid any attention to *King Lear*, he certainly did not take the play's advice. If anything, he became more patriarchal and patronising. In 1610 he explained the origins of kingship in these terms:

> ... a Father may dispose of his Inheritance to his children, at his pleasure: yea, even disinherite the eldest upon just occasions, and preferre the youngest, according to his liking; make them beggers, or rich at his pleasure; restraine, or banish out of his presence, as he finds them give cause of offence, or restore them in favour againe.[8]

King Lear affirms a king's as much as a subject's rights, seeing faults in personal rather than public attributes. Yet we see the debate from several angles, and see tragic capital made of the abstract theory of kingship.

---

[8] 'A Speach to the Lords and Commons of the Parliament at White-Hall, On Wednesday the XXI. of March. Anno 1609', in *The Political Works of James I*, edited by Charles Howard McIlwain (New York, 1965), p.308.

AFTERTHOUGHTS

1

How relevant is it to consider *King Lear* in the light of Jacobean politics?

2

Do you agree with Smith that the 'timelessness' of *King Lear* is 'a myth' (page 34)?

3

Compare Smith's discussion of 'nature' (pages 35–37) with the analysis given in Watts's essay (pages 12–13).

4

Explain the relevance to Smith's argument of the parallel with King David (page 40). How helpful do you find it?

Stephen Hazell

*Stephen Hazell is Deputy Principal at
the Central School of Speech and
Drama, London.*

ESSAY

King Lear as political tragedy

In 1986/87 two productions of *King Lear* in London offered a
particularly rich and instructive contrast in the possibilities
offered by the play, differences both of theatrical presentation
and (consequently) of the meanings the productions yielded. The
first was Deborah Warner's Kick Theatre production in the
attractive studio space of the Almeida Theatre, with the young
Robert Demeger in the title role. The other was David Hare's
production for the massive stage of the Olivier Theatre, with
Anthony Hopkins in the lead. Both directors sought to capitalise
on the theatrical spaces that they in any case started with.
Warner led us into the fantasy life of a disintegrating personality; Hare strongly underlined the disintegrating nation, an
ancient Britain falling into the butcheries of civil war. The inner
life, family life, and the world of politics are not, of course,
mutually exclusive. In our actual lives they bear closely on each
other, and in plays are shown to do so even more (plays offer
something more coherently ordered than three hours in our own
lives), and neither production operated altogether in one domain
or the other. Yet the two different directions of approach to the
play made for very different experiences in the theatre, a
description of which will usefully introduce the main topic of

discussion in this essay: some ways in which it is valuable to view *King Lear* as a political tragedy.

Deborah Warner's production evoked a disturbed and neurosis-laden world, and, as a short-hand description, we can say that it took madness as the issue to focus on. All aspects of the play were imbued with a sense of this madness. Its initial impact was with Lear's appearance in a comic military jacket, playing out what was clearly a childish game with his daughters in dividing the kingdom amongst them. (The element of charade is supported by the text where Lear demonstrably knows the intended outcome of the division before his imperious invitation to his children to earn their portions with words of love.) That this is a father's second, uninhibited childhood is further marked by a playfulness with Cordelia that also has sexual overtones. When the actor Robert Demeger sits Cordelia on his knee to answer the love-question, his obvious youthfulness only increases the sexual tension. Childishly wounded by his pet's refusal to play the nursery game, he punishes her, and turns to the Fool for consolations — physical horsing-about and complicated taunts and tantrums. (The parts of Cordelia and the Fool were doubled; this may well have been the case in the original seventeenth-century production, and there is certainly dramatic logic to it.) Naturally, too, the storm scenes were very mad indeed. The actors effected violent contrasts of light and dark with hand-held spotlights; the only hint of a setting came with stepladders which the characters clambered on (a landscape of the mind, this); rain was simply poured from a bucket; and Lear used conductor's gestures to bring the storm (drum and cymbals) into being. A unified, rhythmic, hallucinatory world was created. All the words of the play were spoken with clarity, yet necessarily, because of the created theatrical context, Lear's words concerning his daughters' inhumanity and perversion struck with greater force than those about the kingdom and its corruptions. Only occasionally did the approach seem to work against the grain of the text; the scene of Lear's reunion with Cordelia ('Be your tears wet?'(IV.vii.71)), which seems inescapably laden with pathos when read, drew no tears from the audience because this Lear remained stubbornly childish-mad and unknowing to the end; there was no moving combination of anguish and pleading here. But it was logical and forceful to follow through the focus on inner dislocation, a strong answer to the question such a rich play puts to the director.

The David Hare version at the National Theatre went for social brutalities. The power game between the generations led inexorably to civil war. The suppressed tension of the acting gave a strong political feel to the presentation: here was a bad system (a greed-society) as well as a power-corrupted king at its centre. The opening tableau of this ancient British court was very still, with the figures physically separated from each other as though each on his or her square of the chess-board; or as in those war-time operational control maps where emblematic armies and navies are moved silently round the map (protecting the strategists from having to face too directly the real bloodshed). Indeed, a huge wooden map of his kingdom that Lear breaks into three is a central emblem of the production, onstage at beginning and end. The stillness of the production was no doubt deliberate. Thus the actors did not communicate with a passionate directness to each other, but wore social masks and hauled to the surface just those feelings that were necessary to enforce their own self-interest. Regan, for example, was presented as in no way a spontaneous human being, but as a silent watcher from whom a social aggression was shockingly released, with increasing fervour as her political control advanced. The central scenes of the play, set in the storm on the heath, were necessarily more physically dynamic. What we were given was a kind of tragic farce of the lives of the dispossessed, both those who have become so (such as Lear, Gloucester and Kent) and those who always were so (the 'poor naked wretches' — III.iv.28 — whom Lear begins to feel for in his mind). Poor Tom, once in society and now out of both wits and covering, was given a particularly demented treatment, the physical contortions quite taking over from the words, as an obverse image to the threatening stillness of the original court scene. The heath-setting involved an elaborate stage-hovel. In these contexts, the social issues sprang out of the words in Hare's production. The minimising of the purely human in the narrative thinned out the expected passion of the play and probably didn't suit the predilections of some of the actors very well — the result was artistically uneven — but the point here is the straightforward one that a radically different significance was produced for the play, without undue manipulation of the text, by approaching it from a different direction.

One final point of contrast. In the Warner production, nakedness became a central emblem for Lear — Demeger spent a good deal of time in nothing but an inadequate boyish night-shirt. The effect, in the specific theatrical context I have described, was one of acute psychological exposure. There was no such stress in the Hare production — the social degradation of a muddy king in beggarly surroundings was clear enough. Rather, the most striking emblems were extraneously provided: butcher's carcasses were lowered over Lear's rioting knights early on and then again over the civil-war scenes. Emotional regression in one case, social barbarism in the other.

My own preference for the 'psychological' Almeida production over the 'political' National Theatre one may reflect the relative strengths of those particular productions or my own vagaries or both; certainly in principle I want to stress the potential interest of politically orientated productions simply because I think we still find personal tragedy easier to compre-hend and respond to, while the other dimension stands more in need of our thinking and feeling through. Having already drawn attention to the theatrical importance of emblems, I should like to examine in more detail what is clearly a central emblem in the text — clothes — as a way of getting farther into the ques-tion of *King Lear* as a political tragedy.

Clothes are, to state the obvious, a sign (whether or not the signal is consciously intended). They can be a sign of social status (robes and furred gowns) or a personal statement (the colour to suit your mood). Whichever, there is a message about the identity of the wearer, all the more so in the theatre where there is little haphazard information. The case that I want to examine here is that in *King Lear* clothes are predominantly used as signs of social identity and much less as expressions of some essential self in each character; and that, further, the way in which clothes become a central emblem in the very language of the play powerfully conveys the political character of the tragedy.

In responding to the opening scene, one of the King's ploys most picked up by audiences and readers is his determination to retain 'the name and all th'addition to a king' (I.i.135) — that is to say, the outward shows, including the robes — while handing responsibility (and hence power) to his two elder daughters and their husbands. Thus is entrenched the fatal divorce between what you see and what you get (you see royalty, you get irresponsibility) that is then capitalised upon by his adversaries (you see obeisance at first, you get uninhibited seizure of power). Less often remarked on are two more explicit references to clothing in this scene. Firstly, there is the coronet that is brought in ahead of Lear and his train. Lear presumably intends to honour his favourite, Cordelia, with this coronet, but then, after she has apparently rejected him, he angrily thrusts it at Cornwall and Albany to 'part between you' (I.i.138); the crown that signified a king's blessing is, by this action, reduced to an empty token, so much golden metal, pre-figuring the reduction of a society, still held sufficiently together by loyalties to the crown, to its broken elements. Then France makes an analogous objection to Lear's rejection of Cordelia:

> This is most strange,
> That she whom even but now was your best object,
> The argument of your praise, balm of your age,
> The best, the dearest, should in this trice of time
> Commit a thing so monstrous to dismantle
> So many folds of favour.

(I.i.212–217)

Here is a rich idea, that our true clothes are the love and respect that others dress us in. It is a deeply personal idea, but also strongly political here. Lear has wanted to compel praise for himself ('Which of you shall we say doth love us most?' — I.i.50) as a purely personal tribute, and his complete withdrawal of favour from Cordelia is precisely because she insists on her obedience, love and honour to him as duties that are 'right fit': she desperately tries to make him recognise the necessarily political consequences of any of his actions, since he appears set on self-gratification only. She points out that the effect of such blind conduct on his part is to generate, not true love, but 'that glib and oily art/To speak and purpose not' (I.i.223–224). Goneril and Regan dress Lear only in hypocritical words. Cordelia's final comment to them on this is: 'Time shall unfold what plighted cunning hides' (I.i.279). Their conduct is plighted, i.e. pleated, folded over, hiding their true intent: to seize power and change the state.

The imagery of clothes, intricately linking the personal and the political in relationships in this opening scene, develops through the play with increasingly explicit social connotations. The unmistakable central image is the process of stripping away. In the first scene, both divesting ('Since now we will divest us both of rule . . .' (I.i.48) and casting off ('. . . with what poor judgement he hath now cast her off appears too grossly' (I.i.289–291)) are introduced. In a process that is the opposite of investiture, Lear unpicks the social fabric himself — he destroys the authority of the political system of which he is himself the pivot, and finds that he unravels rich human relationships in the process (this being why, in a simple sense, the play is simultaneously tragic and political). And when Lear himself is at last naked on the heath, and the kingdom in anarchy, the system itself comes under critical scrutiny. The flow of the play to the end of Act II is the story of the divesting of Lear — its stunning climax being Regan's knife-twisting 'What need one?' (II.iv.259) — and is supported by many references to the disorder of clothes. The Fool, Kent and Edgar, truth-tellers to Lear, particularly bear this message. The Fool constantly stresses inversions: it's Lear who should be wearing his motley, he's only got the crown of his head instead of his sacred one to defend his wits with, he's put down his breeches so that his children can beat him, and so on. Kent assaults the lackey mentality of Oswald, calling him a 'three-suited, hundred-pound, filthy worsted-stocking knave' (II.ii.14–15) — that's to say, his morals are as low as his social origins, however much he pretends to superior status. Kent is outraged 'That such a slave as this should wear a sword/ Who wears no honesty' (II.ii.69–70). A sword is for gentlemen with corresponding virtues — those licensed to kill should be honest men. For his pains, Kent is put in the stocks ('cruel garters' — II.iv.7). Lear then, taunted by his Fool, confronted with Kent's abasement, and fully stripped of his retinue by Goneril and Regan, begins himself to deploy the ideas of clothes and nakedness to understand his condition. He sees, for example, that Goneril's clothes are both unnecessarily fine and, at the same time, provocatively scanty ('Why, nature needs not what thou gorgeous wear'st,/

Which scarcely keeps thee warm' (II.iv.267–268)). He then, on the heath, completes the divesting process, joining 'unaccommodated man', the naked Edgar. As Poor Tom, Edgar steadily emphasises that court society clothes are the coverings of betrayal — 'Let not the creaking of shoes nor the rustling of silks betray thy poor heart to woman' (III.iv.92–94) — while his own nakedness enforces the contrast between a clothed 'sophisticated' (i.e. adulterated) court society and the sufferings of the poor and powerless. He comes in on cue to confirm Lear's own new understanding:

> How shall your houseless heads and unfed sides,
> Your loop'd and window'd raggedness, defend you
> From seasons such as these?
>
> (III.iv.30–32)

Lear's moments of greatest clarity continue to be on this theme, particularly in the climactic scene:

> Through tatter'd clothes small vices do appear;
> Robes and furr'd gowns hide all. Plate sin with gold,
> And the strong lance of justice hurtless breaks;
> Arm it in rags, a pigmy's straw does pierce it.
>
> (IV.vi.162–165)

One of his expressions of rejection of the world of hypocritical power is unbuttoning, and pulling off his boots; another is to dress himself in bitter and stinging plants. Cordelia relays a report of him as:

> Crown'd with rank fumiter and furrow-weeds,
> With hardokes, hemlock, nettles, cuckoo-flowers,
> Darnel, and all the idle weeds that grow
> In our sustaining corn.
>
> (IV.iv.3–6)

Lear makes a deliberate mockery of kingship (he is *crowned* with these weeds) out of the realisation that the order he had thought he saw in society was illusory; the reality was the disorder of unexamined inequalities, the exclusion of the illegitimate, the injustice of the judges. The order of 'Nature' that he appealed to proved to have no binding force. He remains uncertain about his own political responsibility, seeing himself as another victim of the unjust social 'order' rather than as its focal propagator. But the social reversals make him see the instability of the body politic, and discover that there is no essential natural humanity beneath the trappings to rely on. (Nature includes the savagery of beasts as much as the forgiveness of angels.) If the first two Acts concern the divesting of power, and the next two show a bitter vision of society from the angle of the poor and naked, the final Act allows no certainty of the renewal of the former society by humane men: the civil war leads to a depleted kingdom where the political structure it will have is unpredictable and where those that are young 'shall never see so much nor live so long' (V.iii.325). Lear's rage in the second movement of the play (the two Acts of homelessness on the heath) is potentially a constructive anger. The rage dies, and he is 'restored' as far as a child-like longing to spend his days with Cordelia. He is never in any serious sense restored to the kingship before his death. His doctor certainly has him put in 'fresh garments', but the image speaks of the hospital bed rather than the royal throne. When, at the very end, he calls 'Pray you undo this button' (V.iii.308), the director has a real choice: whether he is calling for a life-saving loosening of Cordelia's dress, or whether he feels constricted with emotion at his own throat. Either choice makes for a deeply moving moment, and the point here is that the request clearly recalls, in almost identical words, the divesting of the middle of the play. At the end there is no restoration of the clothed social identity with which he began.

To recapitulate, then: if one follows through the strand of significance concerned with clothes, a broadly 'political' line of understanding emerges. The tragedy flows from the defeat of a man who at first unthinkingly relied on the certainty of a Natural Order (one that would ensure loyalty and cohesion) when only a natural order of politics is omnipresent. Lear's patriarchal and hierarchical body politic — depending on the duty of children to fathers and of the governed to the governors — could only have been sustained by a man who truly understood how to work it. The play doesn't judge whether such a man could have operated such a society with justice and to the encouragement of good; the system is neither validated nor invalidated of itself. All we can be sure of is that, in the world of this play, 'higher' beliefs are desperately close to sentimentality. And since Cordelia is generally linked with a sense of higher beliefs in this play, I would reiterate that it is she who presses home from the start the political points about duty, obedience, and the honouring of contracts, and at the last is still asking of her father, whom she insists on calling 'oppressed King' (i.e. never forgetting his royalty), 'Shall we not see these daughters and these sisters?' (V.iii.7). She presses him, drained as he is, towards keeping the duties of his role. In her we see that there is no necessary conflict between political insight and a capacity for deep love. A full-length study of *King Lear* as a political tragedy would necessarily investigate other topics in detail. Edmund's potentially radical role in the play because he is not within what his society defines as legitimate deserves examination. And the Jacobean context of the play presumably provided a real-life urgency to the subject — it's of teasing interest to realise, with hindsight, that the society in which *King Lear* was written was already set on a course for civil war. But, hoping that the case for a political reading of the play has already been partly made out, I should like to end with a very brief look at the way in which modern criticism is taking up that challenge.

Until this century, the predominant way of understanding *King Lear* was Christian — that is, to see the play as enacting the redemption of Lear through his suffering; to see the basic structure of the play as a pilgrimage to a state of grace such that Lear's love (for Cordelia) becomes the supreme value, replacing the contaminating world of politics. This view has continued to be sustained in this century, but increasingly modified to the values of non-religious humanists. They see the gods as noticeably indifferent in the play, but still see an increase in Lear's self-knowledge and capacity for human feeling as the play proceeds, a kind of spiritual counter-movement to the physical abasement; and assert this as the play's tragic consolation. Both approaches assume that there is something we could call 'essential humanity', something natural, the attaining of which is a good in itself, and which is more important, in the last analysis, than political relationships. Recent Marxist, or 'materialistic', criticism has had to attack this very attractive idea, working from the fundamental notion that human feelings are a consequence of material and social circumstances and are never separable from them. Thus Jonathan Dollimore points to Lear's obsession with his daughters' ingratitude as revealing that both he and they are more vitally affected by what's happening to power and property than by anything else: the idea of family love and loyalties is an 'ideology' intended to keep the power-and-property structure in place, and is only sentimentally viewed as a transcending value.

This sketch simplifies all the positions (Christian, humanist, materialist), but perhaps it can be seen that whereas the first two accept the world as a valley of tears where acceptance of fate and an inner rising above it are good, the last rejects acceptance and insists that we keep our eyes on social analysis. On this view, the play does not achieve an affirmative conclusion, but remains an open dramatisation of a political problem. The responsiveness of an audience is then not only to the personal histories but to political possibilities: ways of challenging repressive ideologies (of authority, family, fatherhood) rather than of taking inward flight to 'human values'. Thus Dollimore concentrates on showing that *King Lear* is 'above all, a play about power, property, and inheritance' (*Radical Tragedy*, 1984, p.197). He reads the moment when Albany cries 'The Gods defend her' of Cordelia (V.iii.254), the moment before Lear enters with her dead in his arms, as precisely subversive of any pattern of consolation; the play's denial of any conventionally closed ending as its great value.

I think myself that materialist interpretations themselves have a disguised set of values — they have to have, after all, a reason for preferring one set of arrangements of power and property to another, and that preference can only derive from a set of human values of over-arching validity; materialists, like most other theorists, take their own most deeply held values as self-evident. But, however much one wishes to challenge them to show their own hand, they have powerfully demonstrated how plays like *King Lear* have been appropriated by essentially conservative ways of thinking that concentrate on individual struggle when there is a large area of political insight waiting to be uncovered; and since the stress on individuality is still the dominant way that critical books on library shelves interpret *King Lear*, I have thought it worth focusing, in this essay, on the way that an absolutely crucial dramatic feature of the work — the divesting of the king — can be seen as insistently political. Critical books can be supplemented by seeing staged or filmed productions, of course, any such production being itself an act of interpretation and implicit criticism. Some of the most striking productions of which we have record — say Peter Brook's version with Paul Scofield, or Grigory Kozintsev's film — show beautifully how far an acute political awareness can deepen, not deny, the response to human individuality in a work of art. But that's another story.

AFTERTHOUGHTS

1

What do you understand by the term 'political tragedy'?

2

Is it better to read a play *before* going to see it?

3

What arguments does Hazell put forward in this essay about the significance of clothes in *King Lear*? How do they relate to the argument of the essay as a whole?

4

What distinctions are drawn in this essay between Christian, humanist and Marxist interpretations of *King Lear*? With which view of the play do you find yourself most in sympathy?

Paul Cheetham

Paul Cheetham has extensive experience as a teacher of English and as a GCE examiner. He is currently a Research Fellow in the Department of Education at Edinburgh University.

ESSAY

The theology of
King Lear

That *King Lear* has much to say about the gods and their influence on or involvement in human affairs is indisputable. Where opinions are sharply divided is on the question of just what the play does in fact say on this issue and in particular what conclusions we are meant to draw about such vexed questions as divine justice and the problem of evil.

The first half of the play offers little scope for significant differences of interpretation; what we are given is the story of a kingdom's initial descent into chaos, precipitated by its ruler's misguided and irresponsible decision to abdicate, the consequence of which is that the forces of evil are unleashed and the King himself is driven mad, thus learning wisdom through suffering in the true Aristotelian tradition. Few people would object to anything in that summary, but when we come to the resolution of this situation in the second half of the play, we find a wide variety of critical responses. At one end of the spectrum are those who see the end of the play as bringing the restoration of order and a sense of divine justice, as good prevails over evil, with Edgar striking the keynote of the play with his reassuring statement that 'The gods are just' (V.iii.169).

There are, however, many critics who would disagree

violently with this interpretation of the play's meaning. One such is the playwright John Mortimer, whose review of the Prospect Theatre production at the Aldwych Theatre in 1972 included the following statement:

> *Lear* and, in my view, *Othello* are about man's suffering at the hands of remote, uncaring gods who use us for their sport, and the human ability to achieve, through adversity and despair increased nobility in the case of the General and spiritual calm and redemption in that of the King. It is because Lear's redemption is entirely human, and found in spite of, and not through, the dominant powers of the universe, that the play is the most moving and important ever written.
>
> (*The Observer*, 11 June 1972).

There is clearly no question of reconciling these two highly divergent views, but by a careful examination of the religious attitudes expressed or implied at various points throughout the play, it may be possible to decide which view is the more tenable and arguably closer to Shakespeare's intentions.

If Shakespeare is deliberately vague about the time-setting of his play, by contrast he specifically invests the opening scene with an unmistakably pagan flavour. When Lear's anger is aroused by Cordelia's reticence, he swears:

> . . . by the sacred radiance of the sun,
> The mysteries of Hecate and the night,
> By all the operation of the orbs
> From whom we do exist and cease to be

> (I.i.108–111)

And later on, when he turns his wrath onto Kent for supporting Cordelia, he swears 'by Apollo' (I.i.159) and 'by Jupiter' (I.i.177). Kent appears to take a more charitable view of the gods when he prays on Cordelia's behalf:

> The Gods to their dear shelters take thee, maid

But in the early part of the play such implicit assumptions about the benevolence of divine natures are swamped by the prevailing view of supernatural powers as agents of punishment and revenge. Time and again Lear associates them with his threats and harsh injunctions. When Goneril tells him 'A little to disquantity' his train (I.iv.246), he curses her with sterility (I.iv.273–279) and prays that:

> All the stored vengeance of Heaven fall
> On her ingrateful top!
>
> (II.iv.159–160)

Later on in the same scene he reassures Regan:

> I do not bid the thunder-bearer shoot,
> Nor tell tales of thee to high-judging Jove
>
> (lines 225–226)

and when he stands on the heath, exposed to all the fury of the storm, he cries out:

> Let the great Gods,
> That keep this dreadful pudder o'er our heads,
> Find out their enemies now.
>
> (III.ii.49–51)

While the use of names such as Jupiter and Apollo contributes to the pagan flavour of the first half of the play, there are also strong echoes of the Old Testament tradition in the repeated references and appeals to the gods as punitive and avenging agents. In particular, several critics have identified in Lear's sufferings distinct echoes of the tribulations experienced by Job (see, for example, the footnote on p.1v of Kenneth Muir's Introduction to the Arden edition of the play.)

Against this stark background one character's views above all stand out in sharp relief — Edgar's. Edgar is the one person who consistently acts upon and advocates the belief that:

> . . . best are all things as the will
> Of God ordained them.
>
> (*Paradise Lost*, ix, lines 343–344)

It is worthy of remark that when Edgar is forced to disguise himself in order to save his life, he does not adopt a simple disguise, as Kent does, but submits himself to the appalling deprivation and mortification of the Bedlam beggars, in which persona he helps the Fool to teach Lear true wisdom and saves his father from despair and suicide. Edgar's reasons for going to such extremes in his disguise are not immediately obvious and are never spelt out, but one possible explanation is that Shakespeare is presenting Edgar as, in some respects, a Christ-like figure who performs a number of crucial functions: by his self-inflicted and undeserved suffering he atones, at least in part, for the vices of others; he inspires virtuous behaviour in Lear and Gloucester, both of whom take pity on him and are moved to show him particular acts of kindness (III.iv.26–27 and IV.i.44); he exemplifies and preaches a philosophy of endurance and trust in God; and finally he leads others to emulate his example, as Lear does when he follows his own instruction to:

> Expose thyself to feel what wretches feel

> (III.iv.34)

On this occasion Edgar is a vital element in the process which leads Lear to learn a supremely important lesson about social justice on earth, reflecting the divine dispensation (III.iv.35–36). Later on in the play he has a very similar effect on his father (IV.i.65–70).

Gloucester is indeed the principal focus of Edgar's moral tuition, and not only rightly but necessarily so, since Gloucester's experiences are calculated to test his — and indeed the audience's — faith in divine justice up to and arguably beyond its limits. When Gloucester defies Goneril and Regan by offering Lear and his party shelter from the storm, Kent remarks, with terrible and unconscious irony:

> The Gods reward your kindness

> (III.vi.5)

Gloucester's reward, of course, comes shortly afterwards, when his eyes are gouged out. And although in a moment of rare insight, when he learns the truth about his two sons' relative merits, he calls upon the 'Kind Gods', it is scarcely surprising that he should quickly relapse into a despairing fatalism:

> As flies to wanton boys are we to th' Gods;
> They kill us for their sport.

> (IV.i.36–37)

Edgar's deception of Gloucester (IV.vi) has the desired effects of curing Gloucester's terrible despair and teaching him dependence on the will of God:

> You ever-gentle Gods, take my breath from me:
> Let not my worser spirit tempt me again
> To die before you please!

(IV.vi.214–216)

and although Gloucester briefly threatens to relapse after the news of Lear's defeat, Edgar is on hand to restore his faith with the all-important lesson:

> Men must endure
> Their going hence, even as their coming hither.
> Ripeness is all.

(V.ii.9–11)

Under Edgar's guidance Gloucester emerges from his descent into despair to a stoical acceptance of whatever life and the gods have to offer. Gloucester learns that there can be no question of forestalling the will of God; one must live out one's allotted span. He has suffered dreadfully, and yet his suffering, which is presented to us so graphically and so shockingly on stage, is used by Edgar in his conversation with the dying Edmund as an instance of God's justice:

> The Gods are just, and of our pleasant vices
> Make instruments to plague us;
> The dark and vicious place where thee he got
> Cost him his eyes

(V.iii.169–172)

and surely we are supposed to see, in the announcement of Gloucester's happy death (V.iii.195–198), a vindication of his son's moral guidance.

The last point is an important one, since one element in Edgar's dealings with his father may make us feel uneasy about his own moral probity — the deception he practises upon Gloucester. The success of his plan to cure his father's despair is entirely dependent on the trick of deceiving him into believing:

> . . . that the clearest Gods., who make them honours
> Of men's impossibilities . . .

(IV.vi.73–74)

have thwarted his attempt at self-destruction, and his success represents a turning point in Gloucester's moral life:

> . . . henceforth I'll bear
> Affliction till it do cry out itself
> 'Enough, enough,' and die.
>
> (IV.vi.75–77)

The justification must be that, given the context of Gloucester's desperate situation, the deception is trivial and in such a case the end justifies the means.

Just as Gloucester learns acceptance and endurance, so too Lear learns the patience for which he has prayed from an early stage in the play (II.iv.269). The Lear whom we see in Act V, scene iii is a man who has been purged of all his arrogance and intolerance by suffering, who has lost his burning desire for revenge and is utterly and serenely absorbed in the society of his beloved daughter. His spirit is not broken (as lines 22–25 make clear), but as well as learning acceptance of his fate he now sees it as divinely endorsed and ratified:

> Upon such sacrifices, my Cordelia,
> The Gods themselves throw incense.
>
> (V.iii.20–21)

Other elements in the second half of the play contribute to a sense of the restoration of divine justice. In the struggle between the forces of good and evil, the advantage is with the latter as far as, and including, the death of Gloucester, but from that moment on, the balance begins to tilt towards good once more. Cornwall is fatally wounded by one of his servants, and the repeated prayers for divine intervention (III.vii), which culminate in Albany's plea that the heavens should send down:

> . . . their visible spirits
> . . . quickly to tame these vilde offences
>
> (IV.ii.46–47)

are answered by the news of Cornwall's death, thus prompting Albany's cry of welcome and relief:

> This shows you are above,
> You justicers, that these our nether crimes
> So speedily can venge!
>
> (IV.ii.78–80)

Act V, scene iii brings the defeat and death of Edmund and the announcement of the deaths of Goneril and Regan, the latter illustrating the point that evil is frequently self-destructive. Thus by the end of the play the wheel has turned full circle, order has been restored, and Edgar, the advocate of an unswerving trust in God, is left in control of the kingdom. In its theological development the play has charted a progression from paganism and superstition through primitive Old Testament attitudes of 'an eye for an eye and a tooth for a tooth' to a New Testament belief in the justice, wisdom and benevolence of God. On the human level too we are assured by Albany that justice will be done:

> All friends shall taste
> The wages of their virtue, and all foes
> The cup of their deservings.

(V.iii.301–303)

Anyone, however, who deduces from this summary that the play presents us with a series of neat and tidy solutions to the major problems of the human condition would be quite mistaken. Shakespeare is far too subtle a writer to distort the reality of human experience by proffering simple answers to complex questions. The play is full of suffering, some of it almost unimaginably barbarous, and much of it strains to breaking point any faith that one might have in divine providence. Kent, in particular, who starts off, as we have seen, with a belief in the beneficence of the gods, ends up a deeply disillusioned figure ('All's cheerless, dark and deadly' — V.iii.289). Overwhelmed by the magnitude of the accumulated miseries he finds all about him, he appears to have no regrets about leaving 'the rack of this tough world' (V.iii.313) and joining his master in the next.

His disillusionment is easily understood, and we may be strongly tempted to share it. To take just one example, before the decisive battle between the two armies, Edgar advises Gloucester to 'pray that the right may thrive' (V.ii.2), but, as elsewhere in the play, the prayer falls on deaf ears. Cordelia's fate presents us with a particular problem. Whereas at least some of those who suffer, notably Lear and Gloucester, have sins to expiate and lessons to learn, it is difficult to see Cordelia as anything other than an innocent victim of sheer vindictiveness.

Our sense of outrage is intensified by the accumulation of imagery which raises her to a semi-divine status; the Gentleman refers to 'The holy water from her heavenly eyes' (IV.iii.30), and on waking Lear describes her as 'a soul in bliss' (IV.vii.46). Albany's prayer for her safety, 'The Gods defend her!' (V.iii.254) is, by yet another of the play's terrible ironies, immediately followed by the entry of Lear carrying her corpse, and Lear's disclosure that he has killed her murderer, while satisfying our sense of justice, nevertheless provides scant consolation for an audience still reeling in horror at the news of her wholly unde-served death. Yet Cordelia herself has already made the point that not merely is there no guarantee in this world that the virtuous will be rewarded, but they may indeed find themselves experiencing utterly unmerited suffering:

> We are not the first
> Who, with best meaning, have incurr'd the worst.

> (V.iii.3–4)

The real point of Cordelia's death is precisely that it is pointless. Like Gloucester we have to learn Edgar's lessons of endurance and forbearance, in the belief that, while evil may triumph for a time and cause almost unbelievable and apparently inexplic-able suffering, it carries within itself the seeds of its own destruction and will ultimately fail. (The point is most forcefully made by the way in which the two conspiring sisters, Goneril and Regan, fall into a state of intense mutual suspicion and end up plotting against one another.) Conversely, while virtuous people may be destroyed, virtue itself is indestructible. It even has the ability to influence the vicious by its example, as is demonstrated in Edmund's change of heart which leads to his admittedly fruitless attempt to save Cordelia:

> . . . some good I mean to do
> Despite of mine own nature.

> (V.iii.242–243)

How then should we respond to the interpretation of the play offered by John Mortimer at the beginning of this essay, an interpretation which can be described as 'humanist', in that it denies or disregards any significant divine interest or involve-ment in human affairs and celebrates instead the dignity and nobility of a man who experiences dreadful suffering inflicted on him by the combined forces of his own personality, circumstances and other external factors? This essay is an attempt to show that, although the setting in *King Lear* is pagan, Shakespeare plots a development from a pagan to a Christian theology, which, dealing as it does in concepts like atonement and redemption, presents us with a divine power whose ways may be mysterious and inscrutable, which may not intervene to save the innocent or punish the wicked, as we might wish, but which is essentially caring and compassionate rather than vengeful and punitive, and without which life would be meaningless and chaotic. In the last analysis it is a matter of faith, but for all the suffering it depicts, the play surely encourages us to reaffirm our faith in — or challenges our scepticism about — the existence of order in the world and the wisdom of divine providence.

AFTERTHOUGHTS

Compare the arguments in this essay with Watts's views on the play's 'theodicy' (pages 13–18).

'The first half of the play offers little scope for significant differences of interpretation' (page 55). Do you agree?

Does Cheetham convince you of the links between Edgar and Christ (page 63)?

Do you agree that the 'real point of Cordelia's death is precisely that it is pointless' (page 62)?

Charles Moseley

Charles Moseley teaches English at Cambridge University and at the Leys School, Cambridge. He is the author of numerous critical studies.

ESSAY

Trial and judgement: the trial scenes in *King Lear*

Hitting a rock before you leave harbour argues not so much misfortune as foolhardiness in trusting oneself to the sea in the first place. This essay, which will concentrate on the five 'trial' scenes in the play, has managed to do something more or less equivalent. We have to decide which 'King Lear' we are talking about.

Most modern editions of the play, like Kenneth Muir's Arden edition which I have used, are conflations of the Quarto and Folio texts of the play. But, most unusually, these are in fact very different plays; both are playable, and it can plausibly be argued that the Folio text of 1623 represents Shakespeare's revision of the play either because he was dissatisfied with it or because the demands of performance made changes necessary. This affects this essay very acutely indeed; the extremely painful scene where the deranged Lear imagines he is arraigning Goneril and Regan (III.vi), is simply omitted from the Folio — as are some 300 lines of Q in all. To us, to delete this scene seems an extraordinary decision to have taken, and its importance to the thematic structure of the play and to Lear's development is one of the strongest arguments for regarding a conflation as the nearest we shall get to Shakespeare's ideal of his play. One could, after all, suggest that the Folio represents a version cut in the light of the experience of the play's reception; it is a fact that Jacobean audiences frequently found madness funny — until the nineteenth century a pleasant Sunday afternoon excursion might be to go with your friends to laugh at the insane in Bedlam Hospital — and this could well have made the playing of this scene almost impossible. The scene skates perilously close to black comedy in any case, demanding that a pretty hardheaded and unsentimental audience come more than halfway to meet it. Jeers and catcalls at this point would wreck the rest of the performance quite as surely as crisp-packets, whistles and burps at any schools matinée. But even if Shakespeare revised the play without such pressure, merely because he was dissatisfied with what he had done, there is no reason to regard Folio as necessarily demanding the ditching of Quarto. Heming and Condell, working members themselves of the King's Men, may well have been able to obtain only what we know as the Folio text when they came to compile the collected Folio edition of the works in 1623; in that circle they were likely to get hold of either the latest text or the text in current use, as revised for acting and prompting. The earlier version was printed at least twice, which does not suggest either immediate dissatisfaction or automatic failure. For the purposes of this essay, therefore, I work on a conflated text, where there are, as I shall define them, five trial scenes.

The scenes I want to look at are I.i, where Lear's charade (I use the word exactly, for the spectacle has clearly been is some measure rehearsed) sets the play in motion; II.ii, where Cornwall, seconded by Regan, 'judges' and punishes Kent; III.vi, already referred to; III.vii, the interrogation and blinding of Gloucester by Cornwall and Regan; and V.iii.95ff, which would have been recognised as a formal and ceremonious trial by battle, where God defends the right. (Old-fashioned even in Shakespeare's day, this remained theoretically part of the English legal system until the beginning of the nineteenth century.) These five scenes all allude to or actually employ the language and structures of formal public judgement whose fountainhead in human society is the royal court presided over by God's vicar on earth, the anointed and rightful king. Necessarily, therefore, they relate to the play's central discussion of the nature of kingship, its rights and obligations.

Before discussing these scenes, it is worth stressing that the first comments we hear about Lear himself concern his misuse of his position as king: despite the intangible and royal quality that Kent (I.iv.32) recognises in him as 'authority', 'he hath ever but slenderly known himself', and 'the best and soundest of his time hath been but rash' — so his 'poor judgement' in I.i hardly surprises Goneril and Regan. It should also be emphasised that a good deal of Lear's thought after his fall begins is concentrated round the idea of the nature of the king's responsibility, as God's steward, for his subjects and the justice of their treatment. But before he reaches this stage, he has to develop a sense of injustice, a sense of outrage at the enormity of what has happened to himself. In the first twenty lines of III.ii, Lear sees the very fabric of the universe as justly outraged by man's ingratitude, which has so signally been exemplified by his own treatment; then, with a sudden shift of mood, his own pain makes him see his suffering in this cosmic upheaval, this cataclysmic storm, as unjust, the elements in league with his daughters (lines 21–24). But by line 49, his thought has raced ahead, while Kent and the Fool have been speaking, to the deeper concept that the storm is the instrument of heaven, caused by, revealing and punishing all the 'undivulged crimes/ Unwhipp'd of Justice' of which men are guilty; the only action left to sinful men is to 'cry/ These dreadful summoners grace'. Yet even with the growing intuition of his own sin, the sense of personal outrage remains: 'I am a man more sinn'd against than sinning'. The word 'punish', which he uses at III.iv.16, is inextricably linked to the idea of what is just; his own suffering leads him to see the failures of his own rule, and he learns pity for the outcasts he has neglected:

> O! I have ta'en
> Too little care of this. Take physic, Pomp;
> Expose thyself to feel what wretches feel,
> That thou mayst shake the superflux to them,
> And show the Heavens more just.

(lines 32–36)

This sense of his own failure as ruler intensifies. At IV.vi.110 the mad Lear imagines he is once more sitting in judgement — and is *pardoning* the adulterer (terrible irony in that context, with the blinded Gloucester recognising the voice of the King); then, later, he perceives that the Justice is a man who is fallible too, and needs pardon as much as the man he judges (IV.vi.151ff). Power and authority is mere accident, and the beadle who whips the whore is as guilty in intent as she is. Too often justice is denied because of power and wealth:

> Plate sin with gold,
> And the strong lance of justice hurtless breaks;
> Arm it in rags, a pigmy's straw does pierce it.
>
> (lines 163–165)

His conclusion, 'none does offend, none, I say, none' (line 170), is a declaration of the mercy that should be solicited from the 'dreadful ministers' by all men, not just the open and obvious sinners in the play. His mind keeps returning to the king's duty of judging with equity and mercy, and to the king as himself a man under judgement. He moves from the assumption that power and prerogative is what makes a king to the perception that it is justice.

This emphasis on justice is not peculiar to Lear. At III.vi.40, Edgar reminds the deranged Lear, even in the court of the mind 'let us deal justly'. Albany sees the justice of the heavens, which seemed to sleep, in the killing of Cornwall by his own servant — the idea of justice is so important that it overrides the normal bonds of duty between master and servant:

> This shows you are above,
> You justicers, that these our nether crimes
> So speedily can venge!
>
> (IV.ii.78–80)

Just before the death of Lear, he promises:

> All friends shall taste
> The wages of their virtue, and all foes
> The cup of their deservings.
>
> (V.iii.301–303)

Whatever our conclusions about the vision of the play as a whole, it is clear that justice is a central concern. Against this background, the five trial scenes can be seen as centrally important. All of them either are public (for justice must be seen to be done), or thought (by Lear in his derangement) to be so. All of them relate in some way to the relation between power, judgement and — in an absolute sense — Justice.

The staging of I.i. is crucial to our getting it in proper focus. All the evidence points to court scenes on the Jacobean stage being played with the utmost grandeur and ceremony; modern productions frequently make this scene look like a visit to the family solicitor. Renaissance princes — and that is what Lear is, whatever his supposed historical setting — simply did not entertain other Renaissance princes in the equivalent of the front parlour. They processed in symbolical and hierarchical order, surrounded by their (planetary!) attendants, to take up positions round the symbolic throne set under the canopy that symbolised the eye and judgement of heaven — and just such a canopy, painted with the heavenly bodies, seems to have been over Shakespeare's stage. This scene must have been visually splendid; if we allow three attendants for France and Burgundy, both sovereign princes, and one each for the Princesses and their husbands — mean by contemporary standards — after line 185 there can be no less than twenty people on stage (including the ominously silent Edmund, who, as a bastard, has no agreed rank in this ordered society). They would be gorgeously dressed — it is, after all, a court — and, according to everyday etiquette, would have been grouped round the centrally placed throne according to their rank. The audience must see the court hierarchically grouped round a Lear who is at the focus of all sight-lines, the man at the apex of the social pyramid, directly by his role linking man to the heavens. The crown is before him. The silent, visual, signals of this scene, therefore, are all of order, hierarchy, stability, and the King is pictured in the crucial judicial role. We see just such symbolism in prints of Elizabeth in her parliaments, or, watered down indeed, in the layout of our own Crown courts.

This scene really is a trial scene: a trial of love, as Lear plans it. Its structure is worth analysis. Shakespeare is not alone in giving us clues to the key areas of his plays and scenes by structuring them in balanced units of lines and time. (This is a difficult idea for us to grasp, but that is no excuse for ignoring it.) This scene opens and closes with two prose passages of roughly equal length, the first telling us — ominously — what to expect to see, the latter giving one reaction to what we have seen and hinting at its consequences. These frame — the analogy with painting is exact, and commonplace in the period — the central block of the grand court scene. This in turn has three crucial moments of action and dialogue, which occur almost precisely at one quarter, a half, and three quarters of the way through. The central lines of the scene are occupied by its climax, Lear's rejection of Kent — a horrifying symbol to the Jacobeans of the divorce of Rule and Reason, from which only catastrophe can follow.[1]

One quarter of the way through, Cordelia refuses to take part in Lear's charade, refuses to flatter him with an elaborate speech that has no meaning; she is insistently linked with the idea of Truth — and is rejected by a father who is less interested in truth than in hearing what he wants to hear. Three quarters of the way through, France, a king who judges rightly, expostulates on Cordelia's behalf. These three points are verbally emphasised: the first hammers home the key idea of 'nothing'; the climax exploits the semantic complex, so important later in the play, of 'madness/ folly/ rashness/ judgement/ sight', and the third lets in the idea of unnaturalness and monstrosity — ironically cancelled and misapplied. We are, in a sense, watching a demonstrative and analytical pageant as well as responding to the illusory reality of a play. Our reserve, our 'deeper sight', is crucial to our perception of the ironic structure Shakespeare has built into the play.

Lear's rightful authority is undeniable. He is a picture of Justice. But the scene (which Lear, a king who loves the grand theatrical gesture, the impressive exit,[2] has obviously stage-

---

[1] The influence of the allegorical Morality plays on the dramatic language of the Jacobeans needs stress; many figures have overt allegorical significance. Kent is recognisably the descendant of the figure of Good Counsel familiar from many political allegories.

[2] As for example in I.i or the great and stagy hyperbole closing with a dramatic and unanswerable exit in I.iv.287. (But after that exit he has to return powerless.)

managed in advance, as the prepared map, the prepared speeches of Goneril and Regan, and the expectations of Burgundy indicate) shows the utter negation of justice and judgement, and thence a kingship that has withered to the mere exercise of tyrannical power for self-gratification. Lear's misunderstanding of what he is allows him the foolish illusion that he can 'unburthen'd crawl towards death' — a king *cannot* cease by nature to be king. What was already a bad expedient — horrifying to the first audience — of splitting the kingdom is made much worse by Lear's hasty action in giving Cordelia's proposed share to her sisters — and the crown, its circle symbolic of natural order and perfection, is given to them to be 'parted' (line 139). But the crucial point is that the charade, acutely embarrassing to all but Lear, is designed solely for the gratification of his self-esteem, as a formal trial of love. A four-part liturgy has been planned — challenge, the daughter's response, Lear's comment, and the award. It is broken only by Cordelia's 'Nothing'. With that word, the whole silly illusion collapses; for love is the one thing that can never be proved, the one thing that has to be taken on trust. Kent's protest, 'Be Kent unmannerly when Lear is mad', shows that the outward rationality hides a madness deeper than anything that comes later. The King, head of the human body politic, has here abdicated his primary responsibility, the ruling of the people committed to his charge with equity and justice. When the head is mad, the body raves.

That raving is soon apparent in the breaking of all bonds of natural duty and affection and the usurpation of rightful rule by mere power. In II.ii, the next 'trial' scene, we see that power in public as opposed to private action. Cornwall intervenes in the brawl between Kent and Oswald to keep the peace — a perfectly proper duty of the ruler. He examines, not without humour, Kent and Oswald; provoked by Kent's 'bluntness', he gives way to anger, and assumes an authority to punish to which he has no right at all. The offence is compounded by his ignoring of the fact that Kent is the King's messenger, and thus by convention partaking of the sacrosanct nature of the King himself. The humiliating punishment of the stocks is gratuitously insulting to the King — as Gloucester protests (lines 141–143) to Regan, who sadistically intensifies it — and a gross perversion of proper justice. It serves to underline the movement of power from Lear to hands which have no concept of its duties and responsibilities.

In III.vi, in the moment of Lear's most profound breakdown, his recognition — visually stressed by his removal of his 'lendings' — of himself as 'a poor bare forked animal', we are presented with the acutely painful mad 'trial' of Goneril and Regan. The chaos of the storm and of Lear's mind has somehow thrown up the memory of civilisation, order and justice and the due form of proceeding. Subconsciously he is seeking to understand what he never tried to grasp in his days of power whose last moments we saw in the state scene of I.i. Indeed, this is a mad echo of that scene; here he seeks a counsellor rather than rejects one, seeks understanding of 'what breeds about her heart', rather than mere oleaginous flattery; he tries to judge, where before he sat attentive to his own applause. But under the memory of what justice and the king's duty were runs the pain of knowing himself betrayed, unloved. This scene's visual and formal echo of I.i underlines the madness of that 'sane' scene and the movement to sanity through madness that is taking place in Lear's mind.

The most frightful of these scenes, however, is the 'trial' of Gloucester (III.vii). Just as III.vi shows how far Lear has moved from I.i, so this scene shows Cornwall and Regan growing in power and confidence in its misuse. Their language indicates their corruption; Cornwall not only decides Gloucester's 'guilt' before the case is heard, but calls him 'traitor' (line 3; so too Regan, e.g. line 37) when by any standards the word must be meaningless. Gloucester suffers precisely for not being a traitor to his king. Sentence is demanded by the sisters with a viciousness that is sinisterly trumped by Cornwall's peremptory 'leave him to my displeasure'. All human bonds and conventions have dissolved; Edmund is sent out by Cornwall with a totally false delicacy, careful that he should not see his father tortured; and he goes without protest. Cornwall has arrogated the power of life and death to himself, even the royal 'we' — the pronoun form symbolising the just and equitable unity of king and people acting in concert (lines 24ff). He is no hypocrite; he knows what he is to do is not justice, but 'the form of justice' — the phrase reminds us of what a trial should be — which he has to follow to avoid offending public opinion too much; yet he is coolly enjoying the fact that he has the power to gratify his 'wrath' (line 26). When Gloucester is brought in, it is Cornwall who stresses that this old man's weak and 'corky arms' must be cruelly bound. Regan asks for the ropes to be tighter so they hurt more. The reminder that Gloucester is their host only elicits deeper insult, a more graphic breaking of bonds in the plucking of his beard. They proceed to interrogate him; but they do not want information, merely something they can use as self-incrimination: 'Be simple-answer'd, for we know the truth'. The questions are fired at him without intermission; and Cornwall's dominance is once again hinted by the way he interrupts Regan: 'Wherefore to Dover? Let him answer that.' There is more than a suggestion that Cornwall is enjoying himself; and what sort of a trial is it where judge is jury and executioner as well? There is no form and order, no ceremony that appeals to a generally agreed ideal of Justice, merely a gross and grotesque travesty of a trial emphasising how unfit he and Regan are for rule of any kind. The plucking out of Gloucester's eyes is almost gleeful, both Regan and Cornwall enjoying the wit of the idea (lines 66, 69–71, 81). This is a terrible travesty of proper inter-rogation in the bad name of 'state security'. Mere tyranny and gratuitous cruelty, the breaking of all bonds of obligation of guest to host, of man to man, have bred from Lear's original injustice. The only — ironic — relief is Gloucester's certainty that 'winged vengeance [will] overtake such children' (line 64); and Cornwall's refusing of all the normal human bonds forces the servant bred up in his household to renounce his allegiance to him in the name of a higher morality. His giving of his death wound to Cornwall — which does not stop Gloucester's second eye being put out — prompts Albany's remark that heaven does indeed intervene (IV.ii.78). But the freedom that men have been granted by heaven means that heaven cannot intervene to in-fringe that freedom, even if that freedom is causing cosmic cataclysm.

Yet legal theory did provide one area for the direct inter-vention of heaven. Evidence, deduction, testimony might all fail to elicit truth, and so the challenge to formal trial by battle to prove the rightness or wrongness of a charge invited the judge-ment of providence on the combatants. The total breakdown of the polity that is imaged in the play leaves at the end no alternative but this last recourse. The duel in V.iii is a struggle between two brothers; right can only reassert itself now through the breaking of the most sacred bonds, which must be sacrificed to a higher ideal. The combat is conducted according to due form, and it is the only trial in the play to be so: the formal challenge, the sounding of the trumpet, the ritual naming, the repetition of the charge. The fratricide is the final image of what Lear has unleashed into the world.

Edmund's fall elicits significant reactions which bear on the idea of judgement. Gonaril peremptorily challenges the idea of right and justice Albany is trying to uphold:

> . . . the laws are mine, not thine:
> Who can arraign me for't?

(lines 157–158)

In her view, power is above moral or legal sanction. Yet she knows the game is up, and having poisoned her sister, kills herself. Her single-minded rational pursuit of what she wants by power has ended in the greatest unreason of all, suicide, the final denial of the self. Edmund, on the other hand, confesses the justice of what has happened to him, and offers forgiveness to his brother. Later — too late — he attempts to undo some of the evil he has done (lines 243ff). He is brought to judge himself, 'despite of his own nature'. As Edmund lies dying, Edgar begins to see some meaningful pattern; Gloucester's appalling suffering through Edmund is linked to his own sin: 'The dark and vicious place where thee he got/ Cost him his eyes' (lines 171–172). The struggle to 'see better' (I.i.158) than Lear did, to 'deal justly', has entailed a descent into an unreason where all structures on which human societies depend have been broken into their constituent parts. The painful and slow piecing together of what is left into some sort of a polity is a task an exhausted Albany, in the end, leaves to an Edgar who has been through the fire and storm, who has begun his political and moral growth with Lear in the depths of degradation and isolation, and grown to something approaching kingliness.

These five scenes have obvious thematic links. There are other connections too. The second and fourth of these five scenes have clear parallels to each other. In both, Cornwall takes the initiative, executing a travesty of justice. In II.ii, we first see Cornwall as a person, green as yet in power. In III.vii, the tendencies of the first are much more obvious, and here Cornwall is not only a tyrant but an appalling sadist. And here he ends, killed by his own servant. The two together are a play in little — the 'tragedy' of Cornwall, a man released into action by Lear's repudiation of his obligations, who causes havoc in the name of power, and turns himself from (one presumes) a perfectly acceptable nobleman into a monster. I have already indicated the echoes of I.i in III.vi, and in them we see a Lear descending into the underworld of his kingdom and the madness of his mind yet groping towards a wisdom and judgement he never knew when he had power. And, finally, I.i and V.iii, the first and last scenes in the play, link in a number of ways. They are, as it were, 'before' and 'after' pictures of a Britain undergoing a cataclysmic purging and cleansing, at huge and appalling cost. They also are scenes of judgement, but while in I.i the forms and ceremonies of judgement are hijacked to the gratification of Lear's whim and ignore truth, in V.iii the human beings have to submit to the judgement of providence. It is no accident that the sub-text of the last lines of the play deliberately suggests to us that Last Judgement when all the graves shall give up their dead. There is a good case, therefore, for seeing these crucial scenes as providing a skeleton-structure on which the issues in the play depend.

AFTERTHOUGHTS

1

What arguments are put forward in this essay about the significance of the trial scenes to the play as a whole?

2

What relationship does Moseley identify between judgement and injustice?

3

Do you agree that the five trial scenes have 'obvious' thematic links (page 74)?

4

What do you understand by 'sub-text' (page 75)?

Richard Adams

Richard Adams is Professor of English at the Californian State University of Sacramento, and the author of numerous critical studies.

ESSAY

The character of Edgar and the structure of *King Lear*

King Lear is by no means alone among Shakespeare's plays in containing telling parallels and contrasts between characters and events, but it is perhaps the one in which such correspondences attain their highest significance. The play's structural interest does not lie merely in the fact of its twin plots — one dealing with the story of Lear and his three daughters, the other being concerned with that of Gloucester and his two sons — but in the affinity and inter-involvement of those plots. For the physical and moral world of *King Lear* is one in which characters find themselves inextricably — and often fatally — linked by situation and event.

In its Folio version, the play comes to an end with the transfer of power from Lear's family, as represented by the King's son-in-law, Albany, to Gloucester's, in the person of Edgar. Nor is this transfer an arbitrary one, as might have been the case if, at the end of *Macbeth*, the throne of Scotland had been made to pass to — say — Menteith's eldest son: rather it is, as we shall see, one for which Shakespeare has been carefully preparing us throughout the action of the play. Edgar is, indeed, the linchpin that holds the two plots of *King Lear* together, and, as such, he has an important structural function within the play. It is my purpose in this essay to demonstrate that function by tracing Edgar's progress from anonymity to sovereignty and by looking, along the way, at some of the similarities that exist between him and other characters.

Edgar gets scant mention and makes no appearance in the opening scene of the play; the focus is principally on his father and on Lear, two wilful old men whose lack of awareness of the true nature and feelings of their respective offspring is about to cause their downfall. With Gloucester, the fault may at first seem trivial: in the course of a brief, informal conversation with Kent, he unthinkingly and without cue jokes about the illegitimacy of Edmund, the younger son who — no doubt to his relief — has 'been out nine years'. Since Edmund's return to court, Gloucester has been so often quizzed concerning their relationship that he is now 'braz'd' against blushing about it. Even so, his confident assertion that the young man will soon be off on his travels again may suggest that he feels some residual embarrassment at the situation. Though we might hazard a pretty safe guess as to what the apparently reserved, respectful Edmund must be thinking about all this, we have to wait for actual confirmation until Act V, scene ii, where he unfolds his plot to overcome the disadvantages of his bastardy and establish himself in the world at the expense of both his brother, Edgar, and his father.

By contrast, we are made to understand the depth of Lear's misunderstanding of his daughters, as well as the folly of his words and actions in relation to them, more immediately. No sooner have the resonantly flattering speeches that their father longs so much to hear passed the lips of Goneril and Regan, than they are called into question by Cordelia's murmured aside:

> Then poor Cordelia!
> And yet not so; since I am sure my love's
> More ponderous than my tongue.

(I.i.75–77)

Lear's youngest daughter warms to her theme when she addresses her father a few lines later. The weight of her love for him is no less than that which he showed in fathering and raising her. It is deep, it is genuine, but it is also appropriate to their relationship. To pretend that it can be infinite, as her sisters have done, is unreasonable:

> Why have my sisters husbands, if they say
> They love you all? Happily, when I shall wed,
> That lord whose hand must take my plight shall carry
> Half my love with him, half my care and duty:
> Sure I shall never marry like my sisters,
> To love my father all.
>
> (I.i.98–103)

Lear reacts to Cordelia's words with an outburst of irrational rage and summarily disinherits her. But his attitude does not go unchallenged. The ever-loyal Kent attempts to 'come . . . between the Dragon and his wrath', to persuade his master to see things as they really are, not as he fondly imagines them to be. And he is banished for his pains. Even the otherwise silent Albany and Cornwall, beneficiaries — through their respective wives — of Lear's folly in dividing and distributing his kingdom, move to restrain the King when he reaches for his sword. And France, whose rank and dignity are no less than Lear's, plays down Cordelia's 'fault':

> Is it but this? a tardiness in nature
> Which often leaves the history unspoke
> That it intends to do?
>
> (I.i.234–236)

He accepts her as his bride without dowry, choosing rather to 'seize upon' her and her virtues than to dismiss them as her father has done. At the very end of the scene, Goneril and Regan demonstrate beyond question that their sister's insight into their characters and motives is all too accurate and that Lear has been terribly hoodwinked. In place of their well-turned phrases about loving their father 'dearer than eye-sight, space and liberty', about being 'alone felicitate' in his affections, we hear them whispering about his 'infirm and choleric years', the fact that he has 'ever but slenderly known himself' and that something needs to be done about the situation — 'and i'th'heat'. Even Gloucester, so blind to the imprudence of his own words and their potential consequences, sees how catastrophic is the state of affairs that Lear has brought about:

Kent banish'd thus! And France in choler parted!
And the King gone tonight! prescrib'd his power!
Confin'd to exhibition! All this done
Upon the gad!

(I.ii.23–26)

Gloucester's own moral blindness becomes more profound and more dangerous during the second scene of the play. It may seem amazing to the audience that he should so rapidly fall for Edmund's fake letter and that he should believe so readily the uncorroborated word of a son who is scarcely a member of his family and whom he has in any case not seen for nearly a decade — but he does. And within a matter of minutes he has been manipulated into a Lear-like rage against his older, legitimate son, Edgar:

> O villain, villain! ... Abhorred villain! Unnatural, detested, brutish villain! worse than brutish! Go, sirrah, seek him; I'll apprehend him. Abominable villain!

(I.ii.71–75)

Edmund's prime motive for undermining the relationship between his father and Edgar in this way is the acquisition of property, power and family title that, as a bastard, he would otherwise be denied:

> Well, then,
> Legitimate Edgar, I must have your land.

(I.ii.15–16)

In this respect he is not unlike Goneril and Regan who, in the previous scene, made use of their 'glib and oily art' specifically in order to lay their hands on as much land and power as possible.

If Gloucester is slower to disown Edgar, slower to pursue his life, than was Lear in rejecting Cordelia, it is only because Edmund keeps him in check. Goneril and Regan convince their father by telling him what he wants to hear. Is it possible that Edmund manipulates *his* father by the same means, that, in some strange way, Gloucester actually wants to hear evil of Edgar? We cannot, of course, know the old man's mind; one thing, however, of which we can be sure is that — whatever the reason for his gullibility — in next to no time he is making plans and giving orders for Edgar's capture and execution and the legitimisation of Edmund:

> . . . of my land
> Loyal and natural boy, I'll work the means
> To make thee capable.

(II.i.82–84)

It is against this uncertain and unpromising background that Edgar makes his first appearance in *King Lear*, at a stage of the play when cynicism and evil are in the ascendant and goodness shows little strength or spirit. And at first he is really a very unimpressive figure: he bends to Edmund's suggestions if anything more readily than did his father a few lines earlier, scarcely pausing to question why Gloucester should be seeking his life. No wonder Edmund can gloat over the good fortune that has presented him with such an easy victim:

> . . . a brother noble,
> Whose nature is so far from doing harms
> That he suspects none; on whose foolish honesty
> My practices ride easy!

(I.ii.176–179)

Edgar scuttles into banishment without attempting to confront his father or check the truth of Edmund's assertions, and with none of the dignity displayed under similar circumstances by Cordelia or Kent. Finding 'no port . . . free; no place,/ That guard, and most unusual vigilance,/ Does not attend', he adopts his Bedlam beggar disguise, replacing the rich attire of a courtier with a blanket barely sufficient to cover his nakedness. He is, in fact, not the first character in the play to change his identity: the noble Kent has already 'raz'd [his] likeness' and become the rough, plain-spoken Caius. But whereas Kent has defied exile and has put on disguise specifically in order to shadow and serve his beloved master, Lear, Edgar's single aim is self-preservation.

It is sheer chance that, having taken:

> . . . the basest and most poorest shape
> That ever penury, in contempt of man,
> Brought near to beast . . .

(II.iii.7–9)

and in that condition chosen to roam the windswept heath-country, Edgar encounters the half-crazed Lear and shares his suffering of the relentless 'persecutions of the sky'. Chance it may be on the narrative level, but this meeting of madmen is also one of the key symbolic moments of the play. Lear, consumed with fury at the monstrous ingratitude of Goneril and Regan, is close to insanity. His rash actions at the beginning of the play have caused upheaval both domestic and political (his daughters, having taken turns to reject him, have now banished him from the warmth and security of Gloucester's castle and will soon be plotting against his life; serious differences have arisen between Albany and Cornwall; and there are rumours of an imminent French invasion) — upheaval that has its natural counterpart in a storm described as both 'contentious' and 'pitiless', and its psychological counterpart in the 'tempest' raging in the King's mind. Lear — well on the way to becoming truly mad — is accompanied by his Fool, a professional madman who punctuates his master's irrational outbursts with pointed riddles and enigmas. Edgar, excluded, like Lear, from Gloucester's castle and in constant danger of his life, is merely feigning madness, but behaves and speaks with exaggerated craziness in his quest for authenticity.

Edgar and Lear share a significant spiritual bond — though a somewhat unexpected one, bearing in mind the play's strong pagan overtones — in that the one is the other's godson. Their encounter on the heath brings about a strengthening of that bond as each learns from his observation of the other's condition. To Lear, Edgar is the epitome of the 'poor naked wretches' in his kingdom of whom he has in the past — as he now begins to recognise — taken 'too little care':

> Is man no more than this? Consider him well. Thou ow'st the worm no silk, the beast no hide, the cat no perfume. Ha! here's three on's are sophisticated; thou art the thing itself; un accommodated man is no more but such a poor, bare, forked animal as thou art.
>
> (III.iv.101–106)

He attempts to remove his own 'lendings' as a demonstration of his essential humanity and as a way of sharing the 'loop'd and window'd raggedness' of the humblest of his people. (In a later scene, Gloucester recalls experiencing similar feelings at the sight of the supposed 'madman and beggar':

> I'th'last night's storm I such a fellow saw,
> Which made me think a man a worm.

(IV.i.32–33)

Edgar, in his turn, is moved by the sight of Lear's suffering to recognise that his own problems have made him unwarrantedly self-centred. While he travelled the country alone, cut off from society, forced to hide from the guards sent out to arrest him, his pain seemed almost unendurable. Now having met someone whose suffering is — if anything — more extreme than his own, he begins to see matters in a different light:

> Who alone suffers, suffers most i'th'mind,
> Leaving free things and happy shows behind;
> But then the mind much sufferance doth o'erskip,
> When grief hath mates, and bearing fellowship.
> How light and portable my pain seems now,
> When that which makes me bend makes the king bow.

(III.vi.102–107)

From this point onward he shuns self-pity and attempts to be more philosophical about his misery. It is better — he tells himself at the beginning of the fourth Act — to be 'the lowest and most dejected thing of Fortune' and to know that conditions can and may improve, than, enjoying happier circumstances, to live in constant fear of some more 'lamentable change'. Confident that he has at last come to terms with his situation, he shouts his defiance at the elements in a manner reminiscent of Lear earlier in the play:

> Welcome, then,
> Thou unsubstantial air that I embrace:
> The wretch that thou hast blown unto the worst
> Owes nothing to thy blasts.

(IV.i.6–9)

Ironically, Edgar is made to realise almost immediately that he has both more to learn about life and more to suffer. When the now eyeless Gloucester, 'poorly led', is brought before him, he confesses that 'the worst is not/ So long as we can say "This is the worst."'

From this point on, his actions argue beyond doubt that he has learned, as has Lear, that the service of others is of greater importance than the pursuit of his own comfort and safety. He escorts his father, who is — like himself — a 'publish'd traitor' and under sentence of death, to Dover, where he persuades him that suicide is no answer to despair. He protects Gloucester when Oswald tries to apprehend and kill him and keeps him in safety while the battle rages between the British forces and those which have accompanied Cordelia from France. He even goes so far as to involve himself in affairs that do not immediately concern him by warning Albany of Goneril's treachery. Finally, he comes, his identity concealed by unmarked armour, to read Edmund a catalogue of his crimes and challenge him to single combat.

Edgar spends a remarkably large part of the action of *King Lear* in one sort of disguise or another. For the majority of the time, of course, he is 'Poor Tom', but then, in Act IV, scene vi, he enters dressed as a peasant to guide his blind father to Dover. His speech, too, alters at this point and Gloucester notices that both the 'phrase' and the 'matter' of his conversation are improved. Edgar insists, however, that he is still the same 'poor unfortunate beggar', and that the only things that have changed about him are his clothes. After Gloucester has, as he thinks, thrown himself from the top of Dover Cliff, Edgar abandons his Bedlam role for good, but still does not disclose his true identity. Later in the same scene, he assumes an almost comic West Country dialect in his encounter with Oswald. His final 'disguise' is that of the mysterious knight who comes forward to champion Albany and demand satisfaction of Edmund. When the Herald requires to know his name and 'quality', he answers that, though his name is lost, 'By treason's tooth bare-gnawn, and canker-bit' (V.iii.121), he is of as noble birth as his adversary. He maintains this anonymity throughout his fight with Edmund. It is important to notice that, with each of his changes of disguise, Edgar comes closer to the resumption of his true appearance and personality. Only when he has developed the moral strength to stand up against his brother's evil, can he say:

> Let's exchange charity.
> I am no less in blood than thou art, Edmund;
> If more, the more th'hast wrong'd me.
> My name is Edgar, and thy father's son.
>
> (V.iii.165–168)

Both Gloucester and Lear have, as we have seen, trodden paths similar to Edgar's in their journeys of self-discovery. Both, like him, emerge at the end of the storm and of their sufferings as wiser and perhaps better men. But, unlike Edgar, they are old and tired. There is little hope that they will live long enough to profit from what they have learned. Gloucester dies, touchingly, in the moment that he learns who it is that has supported and sustained him in his hour of need. Edgar tells Albany how he asked his father's blessing and narrated to him the details of his 'pilgrimage' —

> . . . but his flaw'd heart,
> Alack, too weak the conflict to support!
> 'Twixt two extremes of passion, joy and grief,
> Burst smilingly.
>
> (V.iii.195–198)

Lear, the tempest in his mind at last abated, wakes among friends. Cordelia asks for his blessing, but, instead of giving it, he kneels to her and acknowledges a simple and poignant truth:

> I am a very foolish fond old man,
> Fourscore and upward, not an hour more or less;
> And, to deal plainly,
> I fear I am not in my perfect mind.
>
> (IV.vii.60–63)

He recognises 'this lady' as his daughter and offers to pay the price of the wrongs he has done her. Their reunion, however, is all too brief. Cordelia is hanged in prison on Edmund's orders and Lear dies a matter of minutes later.

It is at this juncture that Albany suggests to Kent and Edgar that they share rule of the kingdom between them. Kent declines; he is physically and spiritually exhausted and knows that he has not long to live. Edgar remains the only person qualified to reign: he is young, but he has already learned lessons that eluded his elders until the very end of their lives. With him as sole ruler, there is a chance that the sick, divided kingdom may be restored to wholeness and the damage wrought by Lear's initial folly undone. Some commentators have found it odd that, in the Folio text of *King Lear*, Edgar speaks the final lines — normally reserved in Shakespeare's tragedies for the surviving character of highest rank. I would suggest, in view of what we see of the development of Edgar's stature and importance in the course of the play, that it is the most appropriate conclusion possible.

AFTERTHOUGHTS

1

Do you agree with Adams that Edgar is 'unimpressive' (page 81) on first appearance?

2

What does Adams suggest to be the general importance of disguise in *King Lear*?

3

How significant is it that Edgar is Lear's godson?

4

Do you agree that 'Edgar remains the only person qualified to reign' (page 85)?

Raman Selden

*Raman Selden is Professor of English
Literature at the University of Lancaster,
and author of numerous critical studies.*

ESSAY

The theme of disorder in *King Lear*

The theme of 'order' is important in many of Shakespeare's plays, especially in the histories and tragedies. In *Macbeth*, for example, the disorder caused by Macbeth's murder of his annointed king reverberates throughout the play at every level, from the natural world to the divine. Shakespeare's history plays show the forces of change at work in the disorder which threatens monarchy in earlier stages of English history. Those critics who prefer to treat the tragedies as expressions of universal truths usually neglect their contemporary relevance. In *King Lear*, it is true, the characters in the play raise questions about ingratitude, folly, pity, patience, and moral regeneration. In so far as modern audiences can share these emotions and values, we can talk about the play's 'universality'. However, major drama is also often addressing its contemporary audience with a special sense of immediate relevance. This essay will place before the reader an explanation of this immediate historical relevance, which will help to account for the acute sense of *breakdown* and *disorder* to be found in the play. The crisis Shakespeare describes is not a universal one (no crisis can be) but one of his era.

In the third and fourth Acts of *King Lear* we hear a great

deal about justice, not merely divine justice, but human — social — justice. Lear's mental suffering — his obsession with 'filial ingratitude' — makes him careless of his own exposure to the elements, but sensitises him to the sufferings of those 'poor naked wretches' who wander the earth unclothed and unfed. Both Lear and Gloucester ask the rich to dispense their superfluous wealth to the poor so that 'each man' may 'have enough'. The question arises — what is the significance of the social criticism we find in this part of the play? Is it essentially a traditional expression of Christian ethics? Or does the anguish of Lear mark a recognition of a real social breakdown, a crisis in Shakespeare's own society?

In *King Lear* the sense of disorder and social disruption pervades the entire play. The storm scenes bring the image of poverty and vagrancy into sharp focus at a culminating point in the action. Lear's anguish in the storm scenes is in part the sign of an insoluble problem. The utterances of the distracted Lear, the disguised madman, Poor Tom, and the Fool, leave us with a sense of disorder which is never really relieved.

The conflict between individuals marks a profound ideological divide. This has been frequently noted:

> On the one hand are those who accept the old order (Lear, Gloucester, Kent, Albany) which has to be seen as, broadly speaking, the feudal order; on the other hand are the new people, the individualists (Goneril, Regan, Edmund, Cornwall) who have the characteristic outlook of the bourgeoisie.
>
> (A C Kettle, 'From Hamlet to Lear', in *Shakespeare in a Changing World: Essays*, ed. Kettle (London, 1964), p.159)

The two groups, as Danby showed, can be distinguished by their use of the central term 'nature'.[1] According to the more traditional view, shared by Lear, Cordelia and Gloucester, natural law is the expression of an order which is both human and divine. Edmund, Goneril and Regan view nature as a purely physical force with no divine dimension.

Shakespeare's dramatisation of this conflict is, as usual in

---

[1] J F Danby, *Shakespeare's Doctrine of Nature: A Study of King Lear* (London, 1949).

his plays, not a simple one. It is tempting to read the play as a conservative tract on the times, and to regard the disruption of the old order as the subject of melancholy lamentations. Lawrence Stone's *The Crisis of the Aristocracy 1558–1641* (London, 1965) shows that the aristocracy was undergoing major internal changes as a result of external pressures, political and economic. The Tudor policy of taming the feudal aristocracy by reducing the size of its retinues led to a gradual run-down of chivalric values. There is also a decline in respect for the aristocracy, which was taken to culminate in the execution of Charles I in 1649. Lear and Gloucester belong to the old culture and reveal both its inadequacy and its attractiveness. Gloucester acknowledges the 'good sport' that produced the illegitimate Edmund. Lear allows his knights to grow riotous, and Goneril complains of their 'epicurism and lust' (I.iv.241). When Regan hears of Edgar's supposed villainy, she immediately links him with Lears 'debosh'd' knights: 'Was he not companion with the riotous knights/ That tended upon my father?' (II.i.93–94). Significantly, Lear defends his retinue not by condoning their morals, but by asserting their fidelity to feudal duty and honour (I.iv.261–264).

When Gloucester talks of the 'ruinous disorders' of the time, he projects them through the lens of this quaint astrological theorising. Edmund's mockery stresses the gulf between the father's older world-view and the son's fashionable scepticism (although one should not forget that belief in astrology was still widespread in the period). Gloucester talks of 'These late eclipses' and their unavoidable 'sequent effects' (I.ii.100,103). Edmund mockingly echoes the phrases with 'what should follow these eclipses' (I.ii.138). Gloucester's backward-looking superstition does not invalidate his sense of outrage, but it does indicate his ideological naïveté, and by implication the incapacity of the feudal nobility to resist the power of the new men.

It was a normal Christian view that social disorder began with malice in families, originally with the strife between Cain and Abel. The Elizabethan homily 'Against disobedience and wylfull rebellion' argued that, as the world's population grew, God extended the model of obedience and hierarchy within families to one of obedience to rulers and governors. Division in families is the play's opening theme: Cordelia's love, which is measured according to her bond, is spurned; Lear disclaims all his 'paternal care'. The treacherous Edmund later apes the true language of filial love when he tells Gloucester how he had reminded Edgar 'with how manifold and strong a bond/ The child was bound to th'father' (II.i.46–47). Just before the storm, Lear, whose foolish division of the kingdom has given his wicked daughters the opportunity to neglect their filial duties, is appalled at Regan's behaviour:

> 'Tis not in thee
> To grudge my pleasures, to cut off my train,
> To bandy hasty words, to scant my sizes,
> And, in conclusion to oppose the bolt
> Against my coming in: thou better know'st
> The offices of nature, bond of childhood,
> Effects of courtesy, dues of gratitude
>
> (II.iv.175–181)

Regan's neglect of hospitality is a fault which has at least as wide a significance as her lack of filial respect. Earlier the Knight reported to Lear 'Your Highness is not entertain'd with that ceremonious affection as you were wont; there's a great abatement of kindness' among his hosts as well as the servants. Defects of hospitality and disaffection among servants are frequently shown. Lear's final rebuff by Goneril is presented in this light: 'I am now from home,' she declares by way of excuse, 'and out of that provision/ Which shall be needful for your entertainment'. And again: 'I look'd not for you yet, nor am provided/ For your fit welcome' (II.iv.203–204, 230–231). The significance of these touches would have been clear to a contemporary audience, familiar with ideals expressed, for example, in Ben Jonson's 'To Penshurst'. Gloucester, like Lear, regards the brutal treatment he receives at the hands of Regan and Cornwall as an offence against hospitality: 'Good my friends, consider/ You are my guests', 'I am your host:/ With robbers' hands my hospitable favours/ You should not ruffle thus.' (III.vii.30–31, 39–41).

Corruption of hospitality goes with corruption in servants. Kent, the true servant of the King, chastises Goneril's steward Oswald and characterises him as the type of the knavish servant who panders to his master's worst passions:

> Such smiling rogues as these,
> Like rats, oft bite the holy cords a-twain
> Which are too intrince t'unloose . . .

(II.ii.70–72)

The phrase 'holy cords' evokes the notion of natural bonds and sacred duties of all kinds. The Fool is clearly thinking of the same kind of unscrupulous servant when he sings:

> That sir which serves and seeks for gain,
>   And follows but for form,
> Will pack when it begins to rain,
>   And leave thee in the storm.

(II.iv.75–79)

Edgar slays Oswald in Act IV, scene vi, and calls him 'a serviceable villain;/ As duteous to the vices of thy mistress/ As badness would desire' (lines 249–251).

Shortly after the first performance of *King Lear*, there were serious enclosure riots in the Midlands, in counties which included Shakespeare's home county of Warwickshire. The enclosure movement had caused disquiet and occasional rebellions (Ket's in 1549) throughout the fifteenth and sixteenth centuries. Most modern scholars agree that during the final decade of the sixteenth century and the first of the seventeenth, there was a marked increase in general public awareness of the problem, among the clergy, the poets, and the politicians.[2]

In the twenty-two years preceding the 1607 Midlands revolt, there were twenty serious food riots, five of which were in 1595, two in 1596, five in 1597, and five in 1605.[3] The growth of population and the development of new methods of cultivation called for more enclosure. The advocates of modernisation and economic efficiency favoured enclosure, especially for grain production, while the Elizabethan statutes (39 Eliz. c.1 and 39 Eliz. c.2) reflect a more traditional and feudal sense of responsibility for the poor, and concern for the loss of husbandry and depopulation.[4]

---

[2] E C K Gonner, *Common Land and Inclosure* (London, 1912), p.139.
[3] A Charlesworth (ed.), *An Atlas of Rural Protest in Britain 1548–1900* (London and Canberra, 1983), p.72.
[4] Gonner, op. cit., pp.155–156.

The neglect of duties by masters and servants (especially the decline of 'hospitality' discussed above) evidently expressed a breakdown of social relations. The rise of the yeoman class is often referred to in the period as a symptom of breakdown. The Fool asks Lear 'whether a madman be a gentleman or a yeoman' and concludes 'he's a yeoman that has a gentleman to his son; for he's a mad yeoman that sees his son a gentleman before him' (III.vi.9–14).

The developing economy was not only directly affecting relations between landlord and tenant, rich and poor, but also subtly challenging economic ideology. According to Tawney:

> The law of nature had been invoked by medieval writers as a moral restraint upon economic self-interest. By the seventeenth century a significant revolution had taken place. 'Nature' had come to connote, not divine ordinance, but human appetites, and natural rights were invoked by the individualism of the age as a reason why self-interest should be given free play.
>
> (R H Tawney, *Religion and the Rise of Capitalism: A Historical Study* (London, 1926), p.183)

Religious and ethical objections to unbridled economic self-interest were continually reasserted during the crises of the 1590s, but more and more the arguments for purely economic considerations became respectable and more widespread. Kenneth Muir, speculating on Shakespeare's attitude, in the early Jacobean plays, to the rising power of money in his society, argues that, while Shakespeare might have coped intellectually with the challenges of such revolutionary thinkers as Luther, Copernicus and Machiavelli, 'the new domination of money was clearly a threat to the conception of order Shakespeare shared with his contemporaries: it substituted for it an order divorced from morality, an authority without responsibility, a power animated entirely by self-interest'.[5]

The tragedies of both Lear and Gloucester are connected with the ownership of land. Following immediately on Lear's unjust and foolish division of his lands, Edmund too announces

---

[5] K Muir, '"Timon of Athen" and the Cash-Nexus', *Modern Quarterly Miscellany*, 1 (1947), p.71.

his intentions: 'Legitimate Edgar, I must have your land'. The 'fierce quality' of his bastardy gives him the power to put aside the customary rights of legitimacy: 'Edmund the base/ Shall top th'legitimate — : I grow, I prosper' (I.ii.20–21). He brings Gloucester to believe that Edgar wants to take over his father's 'revenue', and tells him that Edgar referred to his half-brother as 'Thou unpossessing bastard' (II.i.66). Gloucester's reponse to these lies is, ironically:

> . . . and of my land,
> Loyal and natural boy, I'll work the means
> To make thee capable.

(I.i.82–83)

It seems reasonable to link Edmund with those rising classes who acquired land and wealth by ingenuity and not by birth: 'I see the business./ Let me, if not by birth, have lands by wit' (I.ii.179–180).

The Fool's subtle commentary on Lear's folly in handing over his lands to Goneril and Regan often takes an ironic form. He speaks the language of economic self-interest: 'Nay, and thou canst not smile as the wind sits, thou'lt catch cold shortly' (I.iv.98–99). More explicit is the list of proverbs which include 'Lend less than thou owest [ownest]' and concludes with a comment on the rewards of economic prudence: 'And thou shalt have more/ Than two tens to a score' (I.iv.124ff). When both Kent and Lear mock the Fool's wisdom as a mere 'nothing' of which one can make nothing, he replies 'so much the rent of his land comes to', now that Lear has given it away like a fool.

During the storm, Lear, foolish king and neglected father, Edgar, true son and victim of 'machinations, hollowness, and treachery', and Kent, the true servant, 'A very honest-hearted fellow, and as poor as the King', all take on the likeness and share the life of 'basest beggars'. Edgar, like Hamlet, adopts an 'antic disposition', and studies the role of an outcast servant reduced to beggary. Despite the extravagance of his portrayal, especially his feigned fear of demonic possession by the 'foul fiend', the realism of his conception breaks through frequently. He models his role on his observations of the world around him:

> The country gives me proof and precedent
> Of Bedlam beggars, who, with roaring voices,
> Strike in their numb'd and mortified bare arms
> Pins, wooden pricks, nails, sprigs of rosemary
>
> (II.iii.13–16)

In his feigned madness, he tells Lear that he was once 'A servingman, proud in heart and mind': a wicked, lustful man, now pursued by the fiend. When Gloucester asks what he is now, Edgar gives us a vivid picture of the life of an Elizabethan vagrant who 'drinks the green mantle of the standing pool; who is whipp'd from tithing to tithing, and stock-punish'd, and imprison'd' (III.iv.130–132). Edgar comments on the horrible spectacle of Bedlam beggars who descend upon the cities 'from low farms, poor pelting villages' and 'Sometime with lunatic bans, sometime with prayers/ *Enforce* their charity' (II.iii.17–20 — my emphasis). Henry Arthington, a contemporary of Shakespeare's, believes that the poor often complain unnecessarily and writes of 'their banning and cursing, when they are not served as themselves desire'.[6] Edgar once had 'three suits to his back', like Oswald, who is described by Kent as a 'three-suited . . . knave'. Those servants who lost their jobs and became vagrants had not always been good men. We must conclude that Edgar does not regard Poor Tom as an innocent victim of the new class of negligent gentry. Nevertheless, Poor Tom reflects the disorder of the times.

Edgar's account of the harsh treatment of vagrants is taken from Elizabeth's statute 39 of 1597, according to which a vagabond shall be whipped and 'shall be forth-with sent from parish to parish . . . straight way to the parish where he was born'. Edgar's speeches show a precise awareness of the degraded condition of the displaced vagabond, but retain the point of view of the disguised aristocrat who sees beggary as the due punishment for bad servants and not as the result of neglect by bad masters. On the other hand, bad servants are the counterparts of bad masters.

In the central scenes, III.ii and III.iv, we see Lear's mind

---

6 *Vertues Common-wealth* (London, 1605).

shifting through progressive stages of awareness, from hurt pride to personal anguish and finally to a new sense of the sufferings of others. In III.ii, Lear curses an unkind world and begs the storm to destroy it for afflicting a 'poor, weak, infirm and despised old man'. He associates the anger of the storm with the anger of the gods at sinful men, but excludes himself from the category, being a man 'more sinned against than sinning'. At the height of his self-concern, Lear's mind shifts to a new level which he registers as the onset of madness: 'My wits begin to turn'. His next words are not the words of a king:

> Come on, my boy. How dost, my boy? Art cold?
> I am cold myself. Where is this straw, my fellow?
> The art of our necessities is strange,
> And can make vile things precious. Come, your hovel.

(III.ii.67–71)

Lear understands how precious the simplest things are to the destitute. This realisation presents itself to him as a miráculous change in appearances. He now understands 'true need', its absoluteness and its relativity. In III.iv, Lear's mind achieves its greatest clarity but only after passing through the profoundest darkness of understanding. The external violence of nature is fully internalised:

> . . . this tempest in my mind
> Doth from my senses take all feeling else
> Save what beats there — filial ingratitude!

(III.iv.12–14)

Once again, Lear shakes off his self-concern: 'O! that way madness lies; let me shun that;/No more of that'. As in the previous scene, Kent offers Lear the comfort of the hovel. This time, after a momentary pause and indulgence in personal anguish, Lear announces 'But I'll go in'. He comes to terms, at last, with his humbled condition. He speaks to the Fool with humility: 'In, boy; go, first'. To put it simply, Lear·ceases to be a king and becomes fully aware of suffering humanity:

> Poor naked wretches, whereso'er you are,
> That bide the pelting of this pitiless storm,
> How shall your houseless heads and unfed sides,
> Your loop'd and window'd raggedness, defend you

From seasons such as these? O! I have ta'en
Too little care of this. Take physic, Pomp;
Expose thyself to feel what wretches feel,
That thou mayst shake the superflux to them,
And show the Heavens more just.

(III.iv.26,28–36)

Significantly, Lear understands that the responsibility for justice is man's: the rich must *show* heaven's justice by their action in righting injustice. In Act IV, the speech is echoed in the scene between the blind Gloucester and Edgar. Gloucester begs the old man to 'bring some covering for this naked soul', gives Edgar his purse, and declares:

Heavens, deal so still!
Let the superfluous and lust-dieted man,
That slaves your ordinance, that will not see
Because he does not feel, feel your power quickly;
So distribution should undo excess,
And each man have enough.

(IV.i.65–70)

Both Lear and Gloucester realise that society's injustice demands attention. Their response is not egalitarian (that would have been unimaginable) but paternalistic: the rich and powerful should make an imaginative identification with the poor and wretched and should be charitable towards them.

It seems safe to assume that Shakespeare was aware of the struggles between rich and poor, and sensitive to their social and moral implications. The disturbing social changes which were taking place threatened the validity of Shakespeare's essentially conservative outlook; Lear's painful realisation was perhaps the only possible response. Once we read the play in this light, many difficult transitions, otherwise regarded as the symptoms of madness, take on a different significance. While Lear's ruling-class attitudes can still be discerned in the 'Poor naked wretches' speech, his subsequent madness unleashes a truly radical vision. In Act III, scene vi, in which we see Lear at his most deranged, there are several important references to the disordered world of contemporary England. He abruptly announces the trial of his daughter and appoints a starving beggar (Poor Tom) as 'robed man of justice'. Lear cries out that they escape and imagines them metamorphosed to bitches that bark at him. Edgar, through his tears, preserves his role, drives off the dogs and, shivering with cold, declares 'Do de, de, de, Sessa! Come, march to wakes, and fairs and market-towns. Poor Tom, thy horn is dry.' (III.vi.72–73). These are the words of a vagrant beggar calling on his companions to accompany him on his rounds in hope of sustenance. Lear's next comment goes straight to the heart of the problem:

> Then let them anatomize Regan, see what breeds about
> her heart. Is there any cause in nature that makes these
> hard hearts?

(III.vi.74–76)

It is the hard hearts of the Regans, Gonerils, and Edmunds of the world that make Poor Tom's horn dry.

In IV.vi, Lear enters, fantastically dressed with wild flowers, his mind poisoned with images of lust and hell. He tells Gloucester of the sickness of the world's justice. The judge is as bad as the thief; the beadle lusts after the whore he whips; the magistrate is a worse criminal than the man he hangs.

The sense of disorder in the play is felt at many levels. The ingratitude of children towards parents, the corruption of servants, the decline of 'hospitality' and of chivalry, the chaos of civil order, the cynicism and materialism of the powerful new people, the plight of the poor, and the folly of the representatives of the old order, are all powerfully conveyed in the action and the poetic dimension of the play. As we have shown above, these instances of breakdown are present not merely as universal features of human nature, but as historical actualities which afflicted society in Shakespeare's time. The apparent regeneration of Lear, the stoical patience of Edgar and the saint-like virtue of Cordelia provide some relief and hope. However, the comforts offered by their example are severely restricted. Cordelia's death and Edgar's muted final speech leave the audience with a final impression of a disordered universe, a maimed society, and a world in which the sufferings of the good can only be endured.

AFTERTHOUGHTS

1

What do you understand by the terms 'feudal' and 'bourgeoisie' (page 89)?

2

Which elements of *King Lear* seem to you 'universal' and which topical?

3

Why would an 'egalitarian' response towards society's injustice have been 'unimaginable' (page 97)?

4

Do you agree that Shakespeare's outlook is 'essentially conservative' (page 97)?

Robert Fowler

*Robert Fowler is Principal of the Central
School of Speech and Drama, London,
and author of numerous books and
articles.*

ESSAY

Quantity and quality
in *King Lear*

An audience encountering *King Lear* for the first time might
well be tempted to ask midway through the opening scene just
what kind of people they are meeting, and what sort of world
they are inhabiting. What kind of story is about to unfold? At
first sight, it might well appear after the initial conversation
between Kent and Gloucester, that this is fairy-tale world, a
fantasy or a courtly game. There is a temptation to endow the
characters with the obvious, extreme moral attributes of a fairy
world. Goneril and Regan are the obvious wicked sisters,
Cordelia is the 'goody'. Edmund the bastard has already been
recognised, by definition, as the 'baddy'. The King is an old fool
with blood pressure. France is Prince Charming.

The courtly game which Lear wants to play is a sophisticated, royal example of a family childhood game:

> 'How much do you love me?'
> 'A half-penny, a half-penny'
> 'How much do you love me?'
> 'I love you two pence.'

There are many variations of the childhood game, 'How much

do you love me?' The common feature is the attempt to put a price on love which can be measured in gradations of half-pennies or pennies. Father King Lear wants to indulge in the fantasy of a similar childhood game. Married, secretly discontent and lustful, the father's two eldest daughters are willing to humour their father and to express their love for him in exaggerated terms:

> Sir, I love you more than words can wield the matter;
> Dearer than eye-sight, space and liberty;
> Beyond what can be valued rich or rare
>
> (I.i.54–56)

Cordelia, the youngest daughter, most loved by her father is however unmarried and ready for love, but she will demand a love that is measured by quality. Distrustful of her sisters, she is not prepared to play the childish game: she is not prepared to bid a half-penny. Her reply is uncompromising. What has she to say which can yield her a quantity return of land on her investment of love?:

> Nothing, my lord.
>
> (I.i.86)

The director of *King Lear* will consider carefully the tone of Lear's initial response. Taken aback a little, does he not, with a measure of lightness, at first offer to continue the game?:

> Nothing will come of nothing: speak again.
>
> (I.i.89)

Cordelia is adamant — she will not play:

> I cannot heave
> My heart into my mouth . . .
>
> (I.i.90–91)

She cannot cheat; to play falsely would choke her. It is a powerful image which Lear is incapable of understanding. Looking for quantity, most of the characters present miss the significance of Cordelia's message. The quality of love contained in the heart cannot be expressed by words from the mouth. (Contrast Goneril who says that she loves Lear 'more than words can wield the matter' (I.i.54), then goes on to give a wordy valuation of her professed love.) Only France fully understands.

What is the single event in this opening scene — what is the most significant happening, which sets the play on its apparently inevitable course and offers a clue to the meaning which is particular to *King Lear*, and distinguishes it from the meaning of the other Shakespearean tragedies? What is the 'if only' which, had it not occurred, would have changed the destiny of Lear's family and followers? The game itself has little meaning. The intentions are clear from the outset. The audience know from Gloucester that Goneril and Regan have equal shares. Lear apportions their allotment to them even before he has heard Cordelia speak. It is clear he had already decided which third to give to Cordelia. Although the game is a passing fancy, the meanings it sets up dominate Lear's attitude throughout his voyage of self-discovery. Like other tragic heroes, he constantly reads back-to-front the compass on which he relies to guide him. Thus, every step he takes is in the wrong direction.

A reflecting audience might eventually come to the conclusion that it is not Lear's game, nor Cordelia's silence, nor Lear's wrath, nor Kent's intervention, nor Burgundy's withdrawal of his courtship that closes the door on Lear's options. It is rather the outsider France's acceptance of Cordelia, at the moment when she stands alone with no 'value' but her personal worth, which turns a quarrel over a game into a remorseless, tragic journey.

Lear commences as a man, a king, with a simple and clearly expressed personal need. He wishes to shake all cares and business from his age so that he might 'Unburden'd crawl toward death'. Secretly he had relied on Cordelia's 'kind nursery', the care of the daughter whom he loved most. It is not however in Cordelia's answers that the problem and meaning lie, but in Lear's blind judgement and confusion between quantity and quality. Throughout this first scene, 'worth' is measured by Lear on the wrong scales. France and Cordelia share the values which Lear will, throughout his tragic journey, need to learn to understand. While Lear talks of dowers, bounty, price, power, pre-eminence, large effects, and his hundred knights,

France's own clarity of vision highlights the confusion in Lear's mind:

> . . . love's not love
> When it is mingled with regards that stand
> Aloof from th'entire point.

(I.i.237–239)

Cordelia refers to the material concerns which she rejects and leaves behind:

> Peace be with Burgundy!
> Since that respect and fortunes are his love,
> I shall not be his wife.

(I.i.246–248)

France summarises the topsy-turvy nature of the values of Burgundy and the English court:

> Fairest Cordelia, that art most rich, being poor,
> Most choice, foresaken, and most lov'd, despis'd!
> Thee and thy virtues here I seize upon;
> Be it lawful I take up what's cast away.

(I.i.249–252)

Lear denies France and Cordelia and embraces Goneril and Regan. It is the nature of his tragic journey that the good contribute to his loss of insight and loss of direction. Cordelia's 'truthfulness' disorientates him. Kent's intervention compounds the disorientation. France, by taking Cordelia, makes reconciliation more impossible. Before long the sight of Kent in the stocks will spin Lear round again. Edgar disguised as a madman will be the last straw. The audience can observe these steps as the particular meaning of the play. Man's personal and selfish needs become the need to see the picture clearly and to recognise the needs of all mankind.

The steps are clear, starting with Lear's own selfish, idiosyncratic demands from his position as an ageing monarch, and continuing through to the moment of realisation that all life is about need, and that as king he has neglected to understand this or to fulfil his responsibilities — the needs that others have of him. From the moment of Cordelia's departure his learning begins. Henceforth, if he is to retain belief in himself, he needs to forget what he has done, what he has lost. He needs to believe that his judgement and values were right and that Goneril and Regan were reliable in their protestations. As the awareness grows that they were not reliable, that he has misjudged, he needs the Fool for consolation, although already he has begun to lose the Fool along with Cordelia:

> Since my young Lady's going into France, sir, the Fool hath much pined away.

> (I.iv.71–72)

The hundred knights become a symbol of his need to reassure himself that the contract between Goneril and Regan is being honoured. When he finds that it is not, his judgement is unequivocal:

> Degenerate bastard!

> (I.iv.251)

He starts as a slow learner, quick to disinherit. Soon he discovers man's need to acknowledge his mistakes, and in time:

> Woe, that too late repents . . .

> (I.iv.255)

The quantity of the hundred knights is confused with the quality of love which Lear had been deceived into believing Goneril and Regan had for him:

> What! fifty of my followers at a clap

> (I.iv.292)

is the begining of a declension which remorselessly and logically concentrates the meaning of the play. Meanwhile, the need to keep his sanity, to believe in his judgement and the order of things, forces itself home to Lear:

> O, let me not be mad, not mad, sweet heaven

> (I.v.43)

Meanwhile, the need of the honest to be frank and remedy wrongs hastens the immediate catastrophe. Part of Cornwall's contemptuous description of Kent is not far from Lear's implicit reaction to Cordelia's 'nothing':

> . . . he cannot flatter, he,
> An honest mind and plain, he must speak truth

(II.ii.95–96)

Honest minds and plain, and truth, provoke violent reactions in this story. Plain and truthful speaking results in Kent being placed in the stocks, and Lear further being provoked. Desperately he needs to find an excuse for the failure of Regan and Cornwall to greet him:

> . . . may be he is not well

II.iv.102)

He prophetically descibes his own destiny:

> . . . we are not ourselves
> When Nature, being oppress'd, commands the mind
> To suffer with the body.

(II.iv.104–106)

Shortly Lear will invite his body to suffer in the storm so that he might feel what wretches feel, while his mind begins to disintegrate. For the time being Lear is unable to avoid facing reality and his own misjudgement. When Regan turns the screw:

> . . . I entreat you
> To bring but five-and-twenty

(II.iv.245–246)

Lear tries to remind her of her debt:

> I gave you all . . .

(II.iv.248)

He now firmly equates the number of knights allotted to him with the quality of love on offer:

> Thy fifty yet doth double five-and-twenty,
> And thou art twice her love.

(II.iv.257–258)

Goneril forces him to confront his error:

> What need you five-and-twenty, ten, or five

(II.iv.259)

Regan, who throughout the play is not simply a replica of Goneril but always exhibits the need to go one step further, reduces the question to provoke the answer which is at the heart of the play's meaning — what *King Lear* is about:

REGAN What need one?

LEAR O! reason not the need; our basest beggars
Are in the poorest thing superfluous:
Allow not nature more than nature needs,
Man's life is cheap as beast's.

(II.iv.261–265)

King Lear is about the needs of the living — animal and human — and the realisation of the nature of those 'luxuries' which, it is supposed, make life more valuable and distinguish man from beast.

From this moment of recognition that he has lost what he thought he most needed, Lear embarks on a process, not only of self-discovery but a discovery also of the world as it seems to be. He is identified with nature herself and her fury in the storm. He invokes the elements to discover and reveal guilt wherever it might hide. He discovers what prisoners in the grimmest concentration-camp conditions discover:

The art of our necessities is strange,
That can make vile things precious.

(III.ii.70–71)

He begins to show affection rather than demand it:

Poor Fool and knave, I have one part in my heart
That's sorry yet for thee.

(III.ii.72–73)

By accepting the invitation to enter the hovel, Lear is led to reflect on those who have no roof at all over their heads. Whether the lines are viewed as Christian 'Love thy neighbour' sentiment or political, socialist allegory, the meaning is clear:

O! I have ta'en
Too little care of this! Take physic, Pomp;
Expose thyself to feel what wretches feel,

That thou mayst shake the superflux to them,
And show the Heavens more just.

(III.iv.32–36)

His demand for personal justice has now moved to embrace a plea for the whole world.

Edgar's appearance drives Lear to identify with nature and poverty even more closely as he tears off his own clothes:

Is man no more than this?. . . Thou ow'st the worm no silk, the beast no hide . . . unaccommodated man is no more but such a poor, bare, forked animal as thou art.

(III.iv.100–106)

Lear now needs a philosopher. He needs wisdom, not knights. He has begun to discover himself at the same time as he loses himself. Soon he is also to feel his mortality:

. . . I am not ague-proof.

(IV.vi.105)

Hypocrisy, lust, authority and the wealth that protects evil from justice now become the focus for Lear's anger. He questions the laws which attempt to regulate social man's behaviour to bring it above the level of the animal:

Adultery?
Thou shalt not die: die for adultery! No:
The wren goes to't, and the small gilded fly
Does lecher in my sight.
Let copulation thrive. . .

(IV.vi.110–114)

Why dost thou lash that whore? Strip thine own back;
Thou hotly lusts to use her in that kind
For which thou whipp'st her.

(IV.vi.159–161)

Is mankind worth salvation? An answer to desperation comes later:

Thou must be patient; we came crying hither

(IV.vi.176)

Lear arrives at a point of humility where he needs to beg for pardon:

> Pray you now, forget and forgive
>
> (IV.vii.84)

Eventually, he will be content if only he can live with Cordelia in conditions no better than caged birds:

> We two alone will sing like birds i'th'cage
>
> (V.iii.9)

No longer then — reunited with Cordelia, and forgiven — would he be at the mercy of the ugliness of nature and man; instead, together they could:

> ... live,
> And pray, and sing, and tell old tales, and laugh
> At gilded butterflies ...
>
> (V.iii.11–13)

Finally, he underlines the basic necessity: life itself, without which there is no praying, no singing, no telling, no laughing; no action, no philosophy, no religion, no meaning, no love, no needs:

> And my poor fool is hang'd! No, no, no, life!
> Why should a dog, a horse, a rat have life,
> And thou no breath at all? Thou'lt come no more,
> Never, never, never, never, never!
>
> (V.iii.304–307)

What then has *King Lear* been about? Is it a bleak message, like the definition of life offered in *Macbeth*?

> It is a tale
> Told by an idiot, full of sound and fury,
> Signifying nothing.
>
> (*Macbeth*, V.v.26–28)

Or rather, is *King Lear* like the Christian story, where the hope is in redemption bought by suffering? It is well enough known that the eighteenth century was so dissatisfied by Shakespeare's conclusion (or so unable to accept what the play was about) that Nahum Tate's rewritten happy-end version was preferred for many years. Perhaps a late-twentieth-century audience, who have lived through world events since 1939, are more prepared to view the meaning in part as a terrifying reflection not only on man's inhumanity to man in war, but also on the consequences of greed and lack of care in peace.

While it is legitimate to recognise Shakespeare's special, contemporary appeal, universal meaning is to be found in the lasting quest of humanity for an existence which recognises the basic animal needs but seeks to raise man above them.

The play is about these needs and it is about them on several levels. It is about how man can be either less or more than beast. It is about nature, the nature of animals and the nature of men. It shows how evil can place man below animals and it reveals the constant failure of man to love the neighbour he does not know.

In this context, wants have to be distinguished from desire, selflessness from selfishness, love from lust, need from greed. To accept this interpretation of the play's meaning it is essential to accept that man's nature is susceptible to change, and that goodness will eventually win. The character of Albany — and Goneril's failure to understand it — is significant to this reading.

Lear does not call for sympathy at the end. He at last invites the audience into an objective realisation that, despite the incense of the gods, the brands which separate father and daughter were fired by Lear himself at the outset:

> Hence, and avoid my sight!
> So be my grave my peace, as here I give
> Her father's heart from her!
>
> (I.i.123–124)

> Thou'lt come no more,
> Never, never, never, never, never!
>
> (V.iii.306–307)

Nothing in fact has come from nothing. Death robs life of quality and quantity. Between the initial and final loss, madness and chaos have intervened. The art of the play, the fabric of the imagery, the inevitable and logical progress has given order to the journey. The meaning of the play, what *King Lear* is about, is what both Lear and the audience have needed to learn on the way. Quality care for others and selflessness are first amongst these needs:

> We are not the first
> Who, with best meaning, have incurr'd the worst.
> For thee, oppressed King, I am cast down;
> Myself could else out-frown false Fortune's frown.

(V.iii.3–6)

AFTERTHOUGHTS

1

What distinctions are drawn in this essay between quantity and quality?

2

Do you agree that the crucial event of the play's opening scene is the intervention of France (page 102)?

3

What is the significance of Fowler's analysis of 'need' in this essay to his argument as a whole?

4

Do you agree that 'Lear does not call for sympathy at the end' (page 109)?

Andrew Gurr

*Andrew Gurr is Professor of English
Literature at the University of Reading,
and author of numerous critical studies.*

ESSAY

Albany at the end of *King Lear*

There are two versions for the ending of *King Lear*, depending
on whether the Folio or the 1608 Quarto text is used. In one
version it is Albany, in the other it is Edgar who speaks the last
rather dull and weary lines of the play. If we accept the current
theories about Shakespeare revising the Quarto text, with his
revision appearing in the Folio version, he evidently changed his
mind about Albany, and altered his role in the play. This alteration shifts the emphasis of the play's conclusion quite
strikingly.

From various pieces of evidence it appears that the Quarto
edition of *King Lear*, where it was issued as a single play in
1608, is a rather rough version of the original play as performed
by Shakespeare's company in or about 1605. The version of the
play which then appeared with thirty-five other plays in 1623,
in the first collected Shakespeare, the First Folio edition, is
different in a number of ways, not all of which can be attributed
to inaccurate copyists or printers. The Folio text, it seems, is a
revised version of the play made probably in about 1611. The
fact that some features of the revised text in the Folio are
incompatible with the earlier Quarto version was not recognised
until recently. Consequently editors of the play have tried

to conflate the two versions, and have produced a mixture of the original and the revision. Virtually every modern edition of *King Lear* is an editor's attempt to merge two rather different versions. It will be some time before single-text editions of the separate versions appear. In the meantime we need to look rather sceptically at the conflated editions, and take note of some of the significant changes made to the original in the second version of the play.

In the Quarto text Albany is thoroughly inconspicuous early in the play. Lear's identification and naming of his two existing sons-in-law. Albany and Cornwall, (I.i.40–41) does not appear until the Folio revision. The line which both sons-in-law speak to check Lear's anger against Kent (I.i.161) also appears only in the Folio version. Similarly Albany's hesitant support for his wife when she turns on Lear is emphasised only in the Folio (the lines at I.iv.321–322 are not in the Quarto text). He then remains offstage and almost out of mind until IV.ii. In one brief mention which is in both versions Cornwall unquestioningly assumes that Albany will use his forces to help resist the French invasion (III.vii.1–12). It is not until the beginning of IV.ii that his servant speaks of a change in his attitude. From being Goneril's 'mild husband' he has now become a 'man so changed'. This alteration in his attitude, better prepared for in the Folio where he gets more attention, is noted here in both versions of the play. From then on they diverge. The Folio revision shortens his role considerably. It cuts all the lines which stress his horror and moral repugnance at Goneril's treatment of her father, and leaves him only two comments on the fate of Gloucester (IV.ii.78–81 and 94–97), where he speaks only of justice and vengeance. The Folio eliminates the main expressions of his thinking that appear in the Quarto.

In the scenes that follow, the Quarto gives Albany lines which allow him to justify fighting against Cordelia's invading army. In the revision, the fact that it is a French invasion is minimised, and Albany's debate and his decision to join Cornwall against the French disappear. The Folio text in fact makes the whole story here much neater, by cutting out the inconsistency of Albany swearing to revenge Gloucester and then joining the side which tortured him. The discussion between Regan and Goneril's steward Oswald at the beginning of IV.v about

Albany's support, which is in both texts, thus becomes in the later version a truly doubtful question:

REGAN   But are my brother's powers set forth?
OSWALD   Ay, Madam.
REGAN   Himself in person there?
OSWALD   Madam, with much ado:
    Your sister is the better soldier.

(IV.v.1–3)

There have been hints of Albany's 'much ado' already. Now we know his choice, though we also know in the revised Folio version that it comes from a man puzzled and unsure which way he should move. When in the next scene the Folio Lear rails against his sons-in-law without discriminating between them he can be seen to have some justification. But then, also in the Folio, Edgar discovers Goneril's letters and the plot against Albany. The Folio text makes it much more clear that Albany is a dupe, and Edgar's discovery suggests that he might be saved.

This doubt remains in the revised text for V.i. In the Quarto, Albany's choice about the coming battle, when he is challenged over it by Regan and Goneril, is rational. He will defend the realm against France and ignore the obligations to Lear and his followers. The Folio cuts most of these speeches and leaves the state of Albany's mind in doubt. His choice is now much less an obvious one, seeing that Lear and Cordelia are on the other side. In the event, the Albany of the revised version accepts the policy of the sisters, but with open misgivings. Where in the Quarto he makes a positive, coolly rational choice to stay on the 'wrong' side, in the Folio he hesitates, and his thinking is left unspoken and uncertain.

More than half the total number of Albany's speeches are in the final scene. His part differs radically in the two versions. The changes made to the Folio text early in the scene serve mainly to stress that Albany is now in command. He orders the combat between Edmund and Edgar, and he controls events while he uncovers his wife's plot with Edmund. In the later version he is more visibly upset by the succession of disasters than he is in the Quarto version. The disasters distract him from thinking about Lear's and Cordelia's safety, so that three times he has a chance to rescue them and fails to do so. Altogether, the Folio's changes consistently make Albany clearly a figure of authority but also a ditherer, hesitant, unsure, upset and easily distracted.

At the very end he does the same two things in both versions of the play. They are notably foolish things to do in the circumstances, and they should affect our view of the play's close quite profoundly. Albany is not in any way at the end his country's saviour. If in addition we accept that there truly is a revision surviving in the form of the Folio text which transfers the last four lines from the foolish Albany to Edgar, our view of the conclusion is even more darkened.

The associations of Albany's name put him closer to the crown of ancient Britain than his brother-in-law Cornwall. Cornwall belongs in a corner of the country, whereas Albany's name is close to Albion, the old name for Britain which the Fool cites at III.ii.91. When those other localised figures, Kent and Gloucester, talk at the opening of the play about how the choice of ruler seems to lie between the two sons-in-law, Albany's name sounds the more substantial. As we soon learn, he is also the husband of Lear's eldest daughter (I.i.54), and should therefore have a prior claim to succeed Lear as king. But by then of course we have already learned of Lear's 'darker purpose', his disastrous plan to marry off his third and youngest daughter so that he can divide the kingdom equally between the three sons-in-law — or rather, unequally, since he has set aside the richest third for Cordelia. In the opening scene, Albany has some grounds for thinking that Lear has cheated him of his right. It was an axiom of Elizabethan political thinking not only that kingdoms were not to be carved up, like mere plots of land, but that the eldest son should automatically by the laws of primogeniture be the sole heir to the crown of Britain.

Albany, however, is not the kind of man to grumble. He does not share his wife's angry opinion about Lear's appalling misjudgements and misbehaviour in the way that Cornwall shares Regan's. Nonetheless, he does not take any action on Lear's behalf when Goneril sends her father away. Indeed, he is linked with Goneril in the 'abatement of kindness' of which Lear's knight accuses their hosts (I.iv.60). His passivity through most of the play provokes Goneril, and to some extent justifies her when she calls him a 'milk-livered man' (IV.ii.50), the sort of man who is easily beaten. She has fought for her share of the kingdom, and now plans to provide for herself by cuckolding Albany with Edmund. She is scornful of Albany, an attitude the audience may be justified in thinking appropriate at this point in the play. In both texts it is only at a very late point that Albany at last rises to confront the wrongs that are being done by his wife in his kingdom. In the revised Folio text he is never in control, either of his own mind or of the events in the kingdom over which he comes to be the sole ruler.

By the final scene of the play Albany is the one remaining figure of authority. Cornwall is dead, killed by his own servant who is appalled at his cruelty. Cornwall's wife Regan is dead and with her Albany's Goneril, in their fight over Edmund. France, who offered himself in the opening scene as a husband for Cordelia, and who gave her an army to invade Britain and save her father, never reappears. His title in any case dies with Cordelia in the course of the final scene. At the end only Albany is left with the authority to rule in Britain.

But what does Albany do with that authority? He first attempts to restore order, by returning things to the position they were in before Lear's disastrous 'darker purpose' was revealed. Ignoring the collection of corpses accumulating off-stage, he declares:

> All friends shall taste
> The wages of their virtue, and all foes
> The cup of their deservings.

(V.iii.301–303)

But this well-intentioned statement is a nonsense, as Lear immediately tells him. Dismissing the simple-minded thought that there is any chance of virtue ever being rewarded, Lear says:

> And my poor fool is hanged!

(V.iii.304)

Every word of that searing sentence locks onto the events of the play. The connective 'And' shows it is Lear's answer to Albany's proclamation — How can you say such a thing when Cordelia is dead? 'My' acknowledges Lear's responsibility for his child, and she is 'poor' in material wealth (though rich spiritually, as France says when he agrees to marry her in I.i) because of Lear's actions. She is his 'fool' in her innocence and his responsibility. And she is 'hanged', the punishment for criminals. That alone makes a nonsense of Albany's attempt to give his friends the wages of their virtue. Here and in the next lines Albany shows little comprehension of the scale of the monstrosities Lear has released and suffered from through the course of the play.

Albany's second attempt to assert himself, after Lear dies, is even more uncomprehending. He addresses the other survivors, Kent and Edgar, and invites them to share the rule in his place.

> Friends of my soul, you twain,
> Rule in this realm, and the gor'd state sustain.
>
> (V.iii.318–319)

No doubt he too, like Lear, is weary of the struggle, and wishes to relinquish responsibility for the future. But by doing so he is attempting to reproduce precisely the mistake Lear made at the outset of the play, and which has now finally killed him. Lear's 'darker purpose' involved several basic errors. Above all of them, though, was his plan to give up his own authority, to abdicate in favour of 'younger strengths', retaining the pleasures while giving up the burdens. This abnegation of responsibility, the division of the kingdom, prompts all the troubles that follow. Now Albany is proposing to repeat Lear's mistake, dividing the kingdom once again between two of his nobles, Kent and Edgar. He has learned nothing from what he has seen happen to Lear.

Such a reaction to the deaths on stage is hardly promising for the Albion of the future. It is perhaps fortunate — though none the less accidental — that Kent rejects the offer. Edgar and Albany stand together at the end, the authorities of the future, and one or other of them makes the final statement. Here we return to the alternative versions. In the earlier text, the Quarto, Albany speaks the lines, finally acknowledging that in these circumstances we must 'Speak what we feel, not what we ought to say'. He has twice tried to speak what he thought ought to be said, and presumably has now realised the foolishness of both attempts to assert normality. Now he accepts that speaking from the heart, what we feel, is better than speaking conventionally and offering the orthodox words of authority about friends tasting the wages of their virtue.

In the revised text in the Folio, the words are Edgar's. They must be spoken in reproof. He tells Albany that the conventional words of authority are of no use here. Lear is dead, the innocent Cordelia is dead, and what we feel about that is infinitely more potent than any attempt, however well-meaning, to reimpose a semblance of normal order. Albany was slow to wake up to the implications of his wife's behaviour earlier in the play. Now he is slow to wake up to the implications of the far more painful horror that the final scene confronts him with. He has learned nothing. Albion, under Albany, is not restored to real health.

AFTERTHOUGHTS

1

What differences are there in the presentation of Albany in the two versions of *King Lear*?

2

Do you agree that Albany's wish to divide the kingdom at the end of the play is 'notably foolish' (page 115)?

3

'Albany is not in any way at the end his country's saviour' (page 115). Do you agree?

4

What difference does it make who speaks the final words of the play?

John Saunders

John Saunders is Lecturer in English Literature at the West Sussex Institute of Higher Education, and Awarder in English Literature A-level for the Oxford and Cambridge Examinations Board.

ESSAY

'The promis'd end? or image of that horror?': two different ways of looking at the ending of *King Lear*

When at the ending of a play much concerned with seeing, Albany, the heir apparent to the English throne, breaks off from moralising, with the words:

> O! see, see!

the audience should be all eyes as well as ears. What they hear, Lear's final speech, is likely to be more or less as follows:

> And my poor fool is hang'd! No, no, no life!
> Why should a dog, a horse, a rat, have life,
> And thou no breath at all? Thou'lt come no more,
> Never, never, never, never, never!
> Pray you undo this button: thank you, Sir.
> Do you see this? Look on her, look, her lips,
> Look there, look there!

(V.iii.304–310)

120

What the audience *see* will depend of course — and especially in an adaptation for film or television — on decisions made by the actors and the director.

When Michael Hordern first played the part of Lear on television in a 'Play of the Month' production shown on BBC2 in March 1975, he died at the centre of a tableau, flanked by Edgar and Kent, with Cordelia cradled in his arms. Lear, evidently still deranged, played with Cordelia, trying to coax her back to life. The last of his 'never's seemed to choke him and, following the attempts of Edgar and Kent to undo a non-existent button, his pain gave way to a moment of rapture as with the words:

> Do you see this? Look on her, look, her lips,
> Look there, look there!

he gazed not at Cordelia, whose head was just visible at the bottom of the frame, but above and beyond. There was the strong intimation that he had glimpsed Cordelia in a better world. This moment of transcendence was in keeping with the visual style of the whole production — a *King Lear* directed by Jonathan Miller who had been much influenced by Italian Renaissance religious painting in his choice of costume, lighting and setting.

The ending of *King Lear* has always been controversial. Shakespeare's major source, *The True Chronicle History of King Leir and his three daughters, Gonorill, Ragan and Cordella*, ends with a scene in which Leir and his youngest daughter, Cordella, are alive and reconciled, presumably about to live together, 'happily ever after'. That Shakespeare chose to alter this ending was seen as a dramatic and moral flaw by Samuel Johnson.[1] When he came to edit *King Lear*, he described how he had many years before been so shocked by Cordelia's death that it was only the need to revise the last scenes of the play as an editor that had forced him to reread the ending. Johnson believed that Cordelia's death was contrary to all notions of

---

[1] Johnson's comments on the ending of *King Lear*, taken from 'the Preface and Notes of his edition, 1765', are reprinted in F Kermode (ed.), *King Lear* (Macmillan Casebook; London, 1969).

moral justice. With the deaths of the wicked children — Regan, Goneril and Edmund — it seemed to him as though the play was moving towards a comfortable moral conclusion in which good was to triumph over evil, a triumph accentuated by Edmund's deathbed repentance but dashed by that terrible stage-direction:

> *Re-enter LEAR with CORDELIA dead in his arms.*

Johnson much preferred Nahum Tate's rewriting of *King Lear*, which ended with Cordelia and Lear alive and reunited and Cordelia about to marry Edgar, the marriage blessed by the consent of both their fathers (Gloucester, too, having survived). Tate's version of *King Lear* held the English stage from 1681 to 1838. To Johnson, writing in 1765, it had even then passed the test of time and he marvelled that anyone could prefer Shakespeare's ending. The great German critic, Schlegel,[2] writing in 1811, marvelled that the English could maintain a double ending to the play, 'a melancholy one (Shakespeare's) for hard-hearted spectators, and a happy one (Tate's) for those of a softer mind'. Schlegel was clear in his own mind that the melancholy ending was the right one, finding in Cordelia's death evidence of a moral plan which had evaded Johnson. In Schlegel's view it was right that the wicked should be punished but it was not wrong that the good should die too. However moved readers and audiences might be by Cordelia's 'heavenly beauty of soul', Schlegel believed that it was essential for them to remember that Shakespeare had chosen to set his play (unlike its source) in a pre-Christian Britain, so that both the wicked and the good must be regarded as heathens, not Christians:

> The persons of this drama have only such a faint belief in Providence as heathens may be supposed to have; and the poet here wishes to show us that this belief requires a wider range than the dark pilgrimage on earth to be established in full extent.

In our time, there has been a growing consensus supporting

---

[2] The relevant extract from Schlegel's discussion of *King Lear* taken from his *Lectures on Dramatic Art and Literature* (1811) is also reprinted in F Kermode (ed.), *King Lear*, op. cit.

the view that *King Lear* is a tragedy of apocalyptic dimensions anatomising a moment of crisis in western civilisation when people first had to confront the notion of existence without belief in an ordered, secure universe beyond their temporal world. Seen in this way, the play has increasingly taken on the status of a holy text and critics have looked to the ending to attempt to discover Shakespeare's own interpretation of the crisis, implying that Lear's last words hold the key not just to Lear's destiny, but to our own. Writing in a tradition where Albany might more appropriately have said 'O read, read', critics have tended to fall into two distinct groups: those who have argued that to find any glimmer of light at the end of Lear's (or our) 'dark pilgrimage' would be directly counter to Shakespeare's vision and purpose and those who have sought to find within the play itself evidence of Schlegel's 'wider range' of belief, interpreting the play's ending as implicitly, if not explicitly, Christian in its message. Both sets of interpretations might be seen as a series of footnotes deriving from Bradley[3] who had argued that King Lear should die not in 'agony' with the knowledge of Cordelia's death, but in 'ecstasy' with the 'illusion' that she lives, the ecstasy being manifest in the excited energy of Lear's last lines:

> Look on her, look, her lips,
> Look there, look there!

The key word in Bradley's analysis for W R Elton, an eloquent spokesman for the 'hard-hearted', anti-Christian school of interpretation is 'illusion'. In a detailed analysis of *King Lear* in which he related the play to Renaissance attitudes to providence in a pagan world, he concluded that the play's final moments are ironic, offering not transcendence, but the void:

> In this dark world, the last choruses tell us, we find the prom-
> ised end, or image of that horror, in which man's chief joy is to
> be removed from the wrack of this tough world and in which
> man's pathetic solace is — ultimate irony! — the *illusion* that

---

[3] A C Bradley, *Shakespearean Tragedy* (London, 1904). The discussion of the ending is on p.291.

that which he most loved still breathes: 'Look on her, look, her lips,/ Look there, look there!' No redemption stirs at this world's end; only suffering, tears, pity and loss *and* illusion.

(W R Elton, *King Lear and the Gods* (California, 1966), p.344)

What Lear thinks he sees at the moment of his death has been taken by critics of 'a softer mind', not as an illusion, but as a higher truth. Here, for example, is R W Battenhouse — unimpressed by Elton's conclusions — finding in Lear's last words an affirmation of Christian mystic vision, an interpretation supported by an analysis in which he related the play to the teaching of St Augustine:

> As was true on Good Friday, no Easter vision has yet become available to the sufferers of this moment's desolation. Nevertheless, amid the deep despair there can be (if pictured by an artist of psychology like Shakespeare) occasional flickerings of a transcendent hope to punctuate the moment of darkness. For are not the darkest hours just before dawn, and is not the Dark Night of the Soul the traditional preface to mystic vision?
>
> (R W Battenhouse, *Shakespearean Tragedy, Its Art and Its Christian Premises* (Bloomington and London, 1969), p.288)

Presumably Hordern's death in the 'Play of the Month' *King Lear* would have delighted proponents of the 'optimistic' Christian ending while alienating Elton and like-minded followers who would have seen Hordern and Miller as not being 'true' to Shakespeare. However, in September 1982 Hordern died again, this time in the BBC Shakespeare shown on Channel 1. Again the director was Jonathan Miller. Again the camera focused on a tableau which this time included a fumbling Albany. Again Lear fondled Cordelia like a doll and the final 'never' seemed to stick in his throat. But this time the last two lines were spoken more in desperation than in rapture. They were spoken as Hordern, a much saner Lear, gazed directly at the very dead Cordelia in the centre of the frame. Even if there was a moment of illusion for Lear, there was none for the audience. Behind the tableau a metallic ring of pikes and helmets was more menacing than reassuring. The pessimism of the ending was consistent with the blue bleak imagery of the whole production.

Peter Brook, like Miller, has twice interpreted *King Lear* for the screen, with very different endings. The first was in a much-cut production made in 1953 for American television. Orson Welles played King Lear. When he made his final entry, he dragged in Cordelia like a dead animal, an entry which linked Cordelia's life and death to the 'dog', 'horse' and 'rat' of the last speech, a speech which, to the dismay of purists, completely omitted those most controversial final lines:

> Look on her, look, her lips,
> Look there, look there!

This ending was even bleaker than the ending of Brook's later film (notorious for its bleakness) which was first shown in 1971. The film stars Paul Scofield in the title role. Scofield does speak Lear's last two lines and, though they are spoken more in resignation than in rapture, they are spoken as he falls slowly backward, gazing up and beyond the barely visible Cordelia. In his shooting script Brook asks the question:

> Does Lear see Cordelia's spirit or is this a final madness?

The answer Brook provides is agnostic:

> We can never know.

The two pairs of filmed endings described above are not intended to document a shift from faith to doubt in the mind of Jonathan Miller, or a shift from atheism to agnosticism in Peter Brook, but to show how directors have a freedom from fixed interpretations generally denied to critics. And it is the difference between creative and academic interpretation (not the difference between pessimism and optimism) which is central to this essay. Elton had based his study of *King Lear* on the question, 'What is the validity of the Christian interpretation of *King Lear*?' The term 'validity' is an important one, a 'valid' interpretation being true to the intention of the author. Proponents of both the optimistic and pessimistic readings of *King Lear* claim that their readings are 'true' to Shakespeare. And, though their conclusions are diametrically opposite, both 'schools' reach their conclusions through very similar processes: pointing to patterns in the text which support their arguments, and relating *King Lear* to other works by Shakespeare and to writings of his predecessors and near contemporaries. There is abundant evidence available to 'prove' either case, in the name of Shakespeare. In contrast, Jonathan Miller has said that he prefers to work with the texts of dead, rather than living authors, because dead authors cannot impose their own meanings on their plays as 'valid' or 'true'. In Miller's view, Shakespeare's plays are there to be played with and the players do not constantly need to appeal to the author as a referee. In his own words:

> The only rules to apply are those of aesthetic consistency, formal elegance and accuracy and artistic finesse, and that need have no bearing on what the author actually meant.
> (quoted in Judith Cook, *Director's Theatre* (London, 1974), p.101)

'Truth', for Miller, is a question of the aesthetics of the production, not of the surmised intentions of the author. A somewhat similar position is taken by Peter Brook:

> In everyday life, 'if' is a fiction, in the theatre 'if' is an experiment.
> In everyday life, 'if' is an evasion, in the theatre 'if' is the truth. . . .
> A play is a play.
> (Peter Brook, *The Empty Space* (Harmondsworth, 1972), p.157)

Brook argues that to be 'true' to Shakespeare in performance it is necessary for director and cast to go through imaginative processes similar to those which Shakespeare went through in writing his plays. He also argues that in the theatre 'truth' is 'always on the move'. And here recent developments in textual criticism have unexpectedly leant support to his view. Shakespeare critics have tended to work on the assumption that Shakespeare did not revise his own work, so that in theory it should be possible to establish a single, 'fixed' text for each play as the object for interpretation. However, half of Shakespeare's plays have come down to us in both Quartos (mostly printed in Shakespeare's own lifetime) and in the Folio (the first publication of the complete plays, printed in 1623, some seven years after Shakespeare's death). In some cases both the Quarto and Folio versions are almost identical, the former printed from the latter. In the case of *King Lear*, the differences between the Quarto version (printed in 1608) and the Folio are considerable. However, in spite of these differences, it has since the eighteenth century always been the practice of editors to combine the *King Lear* Quarto text and the Folio text into a single edition. Only recently, in the newly published Oxford Shakespeare, has it been made easy for readers to consider the two texts separately. Here is Lear's last speech in the Quarto version (which the Oxford editors call *The History*):

> And my poor fool is hanged. No, no life.
> Why should a dog, a horse, a rat have life,
> And thou no breath at all? O, thou wilt come no more.
> Never, never, never. — Pray you, undo
> This button. Thank you, sir. O, O, O, O!

> (Scene 24 lines 300–304)

And here is the speech in the Folio text (which the Oxford editors call *The Tragedy*):

> And my poor fool is hanged. No, no, no life?
> Why should a dog, a horse, a rat have life,
> And thou no breath at all? Thou'lt come no more.
> Never, never, never, never, never.
> [*To Kent*] Pray you, undo this button. Thank you, sir.
> Do you see this? Look on her. Look, her lips.
> Look there, look there.

> *He dies.*

Looking at these two speeches as alternative endings rather than as different variations of a common, lost original, enables us to match the texts to 'interpretations' more convincingly than it may previously have been to match interpretations to a single text. The Quarto version, with no glimmer of transcendence or illusion, is tailor-made for the pessimistic school of interpretation. (It was, in fact, the basis of the speech used in Brook's television *King Lear*.) The Folio version — especially if we see Lear's last two lines as an addition made by Shakespeare at the time he was writing his late plays when he was much preoccupied with the theme of redemption — lends some support to those who have found in the ending of the play some flickerings of 'hope' or 'mystic vision'.

The wish that Shakespeare might have revised *King Lear*

was, in 1904, wistfully raised by Bradley (who had a sneaking preference for Tate's ending):

> I believe Shakespeare would have ended his play thus (i.e. like Tate's) had he taken the subject in hand a few years later, in the days of *Cymbeline* and *The Winter's Tale*.

In fact, Bradley knew and referred to both *King Lear* texts, identifying them and conflating them in the second of these two sentences:

> And, finally, though he is killed by an agony of pain, the agony in which he actually dies is one not of pain but of ecstacy. Suddenly, with a cry represented in the oldest text by a four-times repeated 'O', he exclaims:
>
> Do you see this? Look on her, look, her lips,
> Look there, look there!

Strange that Bradley did not see that the 'agony' was a feature of the earlier text, the 'ecstasy' of the later.

There are other features of the Folio ending which support the impression that the later text may present a less tortured, slightly more optimistic ending. Most notably, the last lines are given not to Albany (who speaks them in the Quarto) but to Edgar, whose experiences through the play have paralleled Lear's, leaving him as a stronger, wiser, more convincing leader of the society about to emerge. Though it is difficult to sustain an argument which sees all the changes between the Quarto and the Folio as motivated by a shift from a tragic to a more redemptive vision, the different endings between the two texts and a large number of other substantial differences make it impossible to support any approach to interpretation which posits a single text linked to a single 'valid' meaning. However, the existence of two very different texts of *King Lear* does lend support to those who argue that there can be no 'true' interpretation of *King Lear* which invalidates all others, and that the proper place for interpreting Shakespeare is not the study or the library (though Shakespeare scholarship can be of considerable use to directors and producers), but the stage or perhaps, in our time, the screen.

AFTERTHOUGHTS

1

Is cinema an appropriate medium for plays written for the stage?

2

Brook speaks of being 'true' to Shakespeare (page 126). Is this possible?

3

What important differences emerge between the two versions of *King Lear* is the text of Lear's last speech? What is the significance of these differences?

4

In the last analysis, does it matter how Lear dies?

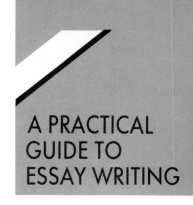

A PRACTICAL GUIDE TO ESSAY WRITING

INTRODUCTION

First, a word of warning. Good essays are the product of a creative engagement with literature. So never try to restrict your studies to what you think will be 'useful in the exam'. Ironically, you will restrict your grade potential if you do.

This doesn't mean, of course, that you should ignore the basic skills of essay writing. When you read critics, make a conscious effort to notice *how* they communicate their ideas. The guidelines that follow offer advice of a more explicit kind. But they are no substitute for practical experience. It is never easy to express ideas with clarity and precision. But the more often you tackle the problems involved and experiment to find your own voice, the more fluent you will become. So practise writing essays as often as possible.

HOW TO PLAN
AN ESSAY

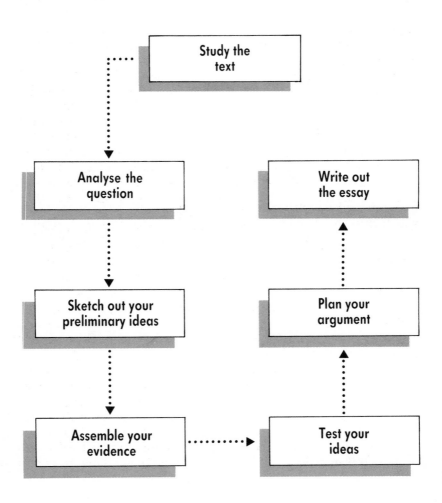

Study the text

The first step in writing a good essay is to get to know the set text well. Never write about a text until you are fully familiar with it. Even a discussion of the opening chapter of a novel, for example, should be informed by an understanding of the book as a whole. Literary texts, however, are by their very nature complex and on a first reading you are bound to miss many significant features. Re-read the book with care, if possible more than once. Look up any unfamiliar words in a good dictionary and if the text you are studying was written more than a few decades ago, consult the *Oxford English Dictionary* to find out whether the meanings of any terms have shifted in the intervening period.

Good books are difficult to put down when you first read them. But a more leisurely second or third reading gives you the opportunity to make notes on those features you find significant. An index of characters and events is often useful, particularly when studying novels with a complex plot or time scheme. The main aim, however, should be to record your *responses* to the text. By all means note, for example, striking images. But be sure to add *why* you think them striking. Similarly, record any thoughts you may have on interesting comparisons with other texts, puzzling points of characterisation, even what you take to be aesthetic blemishes. The important thing is to annotate fully and adventurously. The most seemingly idiosyncratic comment may later lead to a crucial area of discussion which you would otherwise have overlooked. It helps to have a working copy of the text in which to mark up key passages and jot down marginal comments (although obviously these practices are taboo when working with library, borrowed or valuable copies!). But keep a fuller set of notes as well and organise these under appropriate headings.

Literature does not exist in an aesthetic vacuum, however, and you should try to find out as much as possible about the context of its production and reception. It is particularly important to read other works by the same author and writings by contemporaries. At this early stage, you may want to restrict your secondary reading to those standard reference works, such as biographies, which are widely available in public libraries. In the long run, however, it pays to read as wide a range of critical studies as possible.

Some students, and tutors, worry that such studies may stifle the development of any truly personal response. But this won't happen if you are alert to the danger and read critically. After all, you wouldn't passively accept what a stranger told you in conversation. The fact that a critic's views are in print does not necessarily make them any more authoritative (as a glance at the review pages of the *TLS* and *London Review of Books* will reveal). So question the views you find: 'Does this critic's interpretation agree with mine and where do we part company?' 'Can it be right to try and restrict this text's meanings to those found by its author or first audience?' 'Doesn't this passage treat a theatrical text as though it were a novel?' Often it is views which you reject which prove most valuable since they challenge you to articulate your own position with greater clarity. Be sure to keep careful notes on what the critic wrote, and your *reactions* to what the critic wrote.

Analyse the question

You cannot begin to answer a question until you understand what task it is you have been asked to perform. Recast the question in your own words and reconstruct the line of reasoning which lies behind it. Where there is a choice of topics, try to choose the one for which you are best prepared. It would, for example, be unwise to tackle 'How far do you agree that in *Paradise Lost* Milton transformed the epic models he inherited from ancient Greece and Rome?' without a working knowledge of Homer and Virgil (or *Paradise Lost* for that matter!). If you do not already know the works of these authors, the question should spur you on to read more widely — or discourage you from attempting it at all. The scope of an essay, however, is not always so obvious and you must remain alert to the implied demands of each question. How could you possibly 'Consider the view that *Wuthering Heights* transcends the conventions of the Gothic novel' without reference to at least some of those works which, the question suggests, have *not* transcended Gothic conventions?

When you have decided on a topic, analyse the terms of the question itself. Sometimes these self-evidently require careful definition: *tragedy* and *irony*, for example, are notoriously difficult concepts to pin down and you will probably need to consult a good dictionary of literary terms. Don't ignore, however, those seemingly innocuous phrases which often smuggle in significant assumptions. 'Does Macbeth lack the nobility of the true tragic hero?' obviously invites you to discuss nobility and the nature of the tragic hero. But what of 'lack' and 'true' — do they suggest that the play would be improved had Shakespeare depicted Macbeth in a different manner? or that tragedy is superior to other forms of drama? Remember that you are not expected meekly to agree with the assumptions implicit in the question. Some questions are deliberately provocative in order to stimulate an engaged response. Don't be afraid to take up the challenge.

Sketch out your preliminary ideas

'Which comes first, the evidence or the answer?' is one of those chicken and egg questions. How can you form a view without inspecting the evidence? But how can you know which evidence is relevant without some idea of what it is you are looking for? In practice the mind reviews evidence and formulates preliminary theories or hypotheses at one and the same time, although for the sake of clarity we have separated out the processes. Remember that these early ideas are only there to get you started. You *expect* to modify them in the light of the evidence you uncover. Your initial hypothesis may be an instinctive 'gut-reaction'. Or you may find that you prefer to 'sleep on the problem', allowing ideas to gell over a period of time. Don't worry in either case. The mind is quite capable of processing a vast amount of accumulated evidence, the product of previous reading and thought, and reaching sophisticated intuitive judgements. Eventually, however, you are going to have to think carefully through any ideas you arrive at by such intuitive processes. Are they logical? Do they take account of all the relevant factors? Do they fully answer the question set? Are there any obvious reasons to qualify or abandon them?

Assemble your evidence

Now is the time to return to the text and re-read it with the question and your working hypothesis firmly in mind. Many of the notes you have already made are likely to be useful, but assess the precise relevance of this material and make notes on any new evidence you discover. The important thing is to cast your net widely and take into account points which tend to undermine your case as well as those that support it. As always, ensure that your notes are full, accurate, and reflect your own critical judgements.

You may well need to go outside the text if you are to do full justice to the question. If you think that the 'Oedipus complex' may be relevant to an answer on *Hamlet* then read Freud and a balanced selection of those critics who have discussed the appropriateness of applying psychoanalytical theories to the interpretation of literature. Their views can most easily be tracked down by consulting the annotated bibliographies held by most major libraries (and don't be afraid to ask a librarian for help in finding and using these). Remember that you go to works of criticism not only to obtain information but to stimulate you into clarifying your own position. And that since life is short and many critical studies are long, judicious use of a book's index and/or contents list is not to be scorned. You can save yourself a great deal of future labour if you care-fully record full bibliographic details at this stage.

Once you have collected the evidence, organise it coher-ently. Sort the detailed points into related groups and identify the quotations which support these. You must also assess the relative importance of each point, for in an essay of limited length it is essential to establish a firm set of priorities, exploring some ideas in depth while discarding or subordinating others.

Test your ideas

As we stressed earlier, a hypothesis is only a proposal, and one that you fully expect to modify. Review it with the evidence before you. Do you really still believe in it? It would be surprising if you did not want to modify it in some way. If you cannot see any problems, others may. Try discussing your ideas with friends and relatives. Raise them in class discussions. Your tutor is certain to welcome your initiative. The critical process is essentially collaborative and there is absolutely no reason why you should not listen to and benefit from the views of others. Similarly, you should feel free to test your ideas against the theories put forward in academic journals and books. But do not just borrow what you find. Critically analyse the views on offer and, where appropriate, integrate them into your own pattern of thought. You must, of course, give full acknowledgement to the sources of such views.

Do not despair if you find you have to abandon or modify significantly your initial position. The fact that you are prepared to do so is a mark of intellectual integrity. Dogmatism is never an academic virtue and many of the best essays explore the *process* of scholarly enquiry rather than simply record its results.

Plan your argument

Once you have more or less decided on your attitude to the question (for an answer is never really 'finalised') you have to present your case in the most persuasive manner. In order to do this you must avoid meandering from point to point and instead produce an organised argument — a structured flow of ideas and supporting evidence, leading logically to a conclusion which fully answers the question. Never begin to write until you have produced an outline of your argument.

You may find it easiest to begin by sketching out its main stage as a flow chart or some other form of visual presentation. But eventually you should produce a list of paragraph topics. The paragraph is the conventional written demarcation for a unit of thought and you can outline an argument quite simply by briefly summarising the substance of each paragraph and then checking that these points (you may remember your English teacher referring to them as topic sentences) really do follow a coherent order. Later you will be able to elaborate on each topic, illustrating and qualifying it as you go along. But you will find this far easier to do if you possess from the outset a clear map of where you are heading.

All questions require some form of an argument. Even so-called 'descriptive' questions *imply* the need for an argument. An adequate answer to the request to 'Outline the role of Iago in *Othello*' would do far more than simply list his appearances on stage. It would at the very least attempt to provide some *explanation* for his actions — is he, for example, a representative stage 'Machiavel'? an example of pure evil, 'motiveless malignity'? or a realistic study of a tormented personality reacting to identifiable social and psychological pressures?

Your conclusion ought to address the terms of the question. It may seem obvious, but 'how far do you agree', 'evaluate', 'consider', 'discuss', etc, are *not* interchangeable formulas and your conclusion must take account of the precise wording of the question. If asked 'How far do you agree?', the concluding paragraph of your essay really should state whether you are in complete agreement, total disagreement, or, more likely, partial agreement. Each preceding paragraph should have a clear justification for its existence and help to clarify the reasoning which underlies your conclusion. If you find that a paragraph serves no good purpose (perhaps merely summarising the plot), do not hesitate to discard it.

The arrangement of the paragraphs, the overall strategy of the argument, can vary. One possible pattern is dialectical: present the arguments in favour of one point of view (**thesis**); then turn to counter-arguments or to a rival interpretation (**antithesis**); finally evaluate the competing claims and arrive at your own conclusion (**synthesis**). You may, on the other hand, feel so convinced of the merits of one particular case that you wish to devote your entire essay to arguing that viewpoint persuasively (although it is always desirable to indicate, however briefly, that you are aware of alternative, if flawed, positions). As the essays contained in this volume demonstrate, there are many other possible strategies. Try to adopt the one which will most comfortably accommodate the demands of the question and allow you to express your thoughts with the greatest possible clarity.

Be careful, however, not to apply abstract formulas in a mechanical manner. It is true that you should be careful to define your terms. It is *not* true that every essay should begin with 'The dictionary defines x as . . .'. In fact, definitions are often best left until an appropriate moment for their introduction arrives. Similarly every essay should have a beginning, middle and end. But it does not follow that in your opening paragraph you should announce an intention to write an essay, or that in your concluding paragraph you need to signal an imminent desire to put down your pen. The old adages are often useful reminders of what constitutes good practice, but they must be interpreted intelligently.

Write out the essay

Once you have developed a coherent argument you should aim to communicate it in the most effective manner possible. Make certain you clearly identify yourself, and the question you are answering. Ideally, type your answer, or at least ensure your handwriting is legible and that you leave sufficient space for your tutor's comments. Careless presentation merely distracts from the force of your argument. Errors of grammar, syntax and spelling are far more serious. At best they are an irritating blemish, particularly in the work of a student who should be sensitive to the nuances of language. At worst, they seriously confuse the sense of your argument. If you are aware that you have stylistic problems of this kind, ask your tutor for advice at the earliest opportunity. Everyone, however, is liable to commit the occasional howler. The only remedy is to give yourself plenty of time in which to proof-read your manuscript (often reading it aloud is helpful) before submitting it.

Language, however, is not only an instrument of communication; it is also an instrument of thought. If you want to think clearly and precisely you should strive for a clear, precise prose style. Keep your sentences short and direct. Use modern, straightforward English wherever possible. Avoid repetition, clichés and wordiness. Beware of generalisations, simplifications, and overstatements. Orwell analysed the relationship between stylistic vice and muddled thought in his essay 'Politics and the English Language' (1946) — it remains essential reading (and is still readily available in volume 4 of the Penguin *Collected Essays, Journalism and Letters*). Generalisations, for example, are always dangerous. They are rarely true and tend to suppress the individuality of the texts in question. A remark such as 'Keats always employs sensuous language in his poetry' is not only fatuous (what, after all, does it mean? is *every* word he wrote equally 'sensuous'?) but tends to obscure interesting distinctions which could otherwise be made between, say, the descriptions in the 'Ode on a Grecian Urn' and those in 'To Autumn'.

The intelligent use of quotations can help you make your points with greater clarity. Don't sprinkle them throughout your essay without good reason. There is no need, for example, to use them to support uncontentious statements of fact. 'Macbeth murdered Duncan' does not require textual evidence (unless you wish to dispute Thurber's brilliant parody, 'The Great Macbeth Murder Mystery', which reveals Lady Macbeth's father as the culprit!). Quotations should be included, however, when they are necessary to support your case. The proposition that Macbeth's imaginative powers wither after he has killed his king would certainly require extensive quotation: you would almost certainly want to analyse key passages from both before and after the murder (perhaps his first and last soliloquies?). The key word here is 'analyse'. Quotations cannot make your points on their own. It is up to you to demonstrate their relevance and clearly explain to your readers *why* you want them to focus on the passage you have selected.

Most of the academic conventions which govern the presentation of essays are set out briefly in the style sheet below. The question of gender, however, requires fuller discussion. More than half the population of the world is female. Yet many writers still refer to an undifferentiated *man*kind. Or write of the author and *his* public. We do not think that this convention has much to recommend it. At the very least, it runs the risk of introducing unintended sexist attitudes. And at times leads to such patent absurdities as 'Cleopatra's final speech asserts *man*'s true nobility'. With a little thought, you can normally find ways of expressing yourself which do not suggest that the typical author, critic or reader is male. Often you can simply use plural forms, which is probably a more elegant solution than relying on such awkward formulations as 's/he' or 'he and she'. You should also try to avoid distinguishing between male and female authors on the basis of forenames. Why *Jane* Austen and not *George* Byron? Refer to all authors by their last names unless there is some good reason not to. Where there may otherwise be confusion, say between T S and George Eliot, give the name in full when it first occurs and thereafter use the last name only.

Finally, keep your audience firmly in mind. Tutors and examiners are interested in understanding your conclusions and the processes by which you arrived at them. They are not interested in reading a potted version of a book they already know. **So don't pad out your work with plot summary.**

Hints for examinations

In an examination you should go through exactly the same processes as you would for the preparation of a term essay. The only difference lies in the fact that some of the stages will have had to take place before you enter the examination room. This should not bother you unduly. Examiners are bound to avoid the merely eccentric when they come to formulate papers and if you have read widely and thought deeply about the central issues raised by your set texts you can be confident you will have sufficient material to answer the majority of questions sensibly.

The fact that examinations impose strict time limits makes it *more* rather than less, important that you plan carefully. There really is no point in floundering into an answer without any idea of where you are going, particularly when there will not be time to recover from the initial error.

Before you begin to answer any question at all, study the entire paper with care. Check that you understand the rubric and know how many questions you have to answer and whether any are compulsory. It may be comforting to spot a title you feel confident of answering well, but don't rush to tackle it: read *all* the questions before deciding which *combination* will allow you to display your abilities to the fullest advantage. Once you have made your choice, analyse each question, sketch out your ideas, assemble the evidence, review your initial hypothesis, play your argument, *before* trying to write out an answer. And make notes at each stage: not only will these help you arrive at a sensible conclusion, but examiners are impressed by evidence of careful thought.

Plan your time as well as your answers. If you have practised writing timed essays as part of your revision, you should not find this too difficult. There can be a temptation to allocate extra time to the questions you know you can answer well; but this is always a short-sighted policy. You will find yourself left to face a question which would in any event have given you difficulty without even the time to give it serious thought. It is, moreover, easier to gain marks at the lower end of the scale than at the upper, and you will never compensate for one poor answer by further polishing two satisfactory answers. Try to leave some time at the end of the examination to re-read your answers and correct any obvious errors. If the worst comes to the worst and you run short of time, don't just keep writing until you are forced to break off in mid-paragraph. It is far better to provide for the examiner a set of notes which indicate the overall direction of your argument.

Good luck — but if you prepare for the examination conscientiously and tackle the paper in a methodical manner, you won't need it!

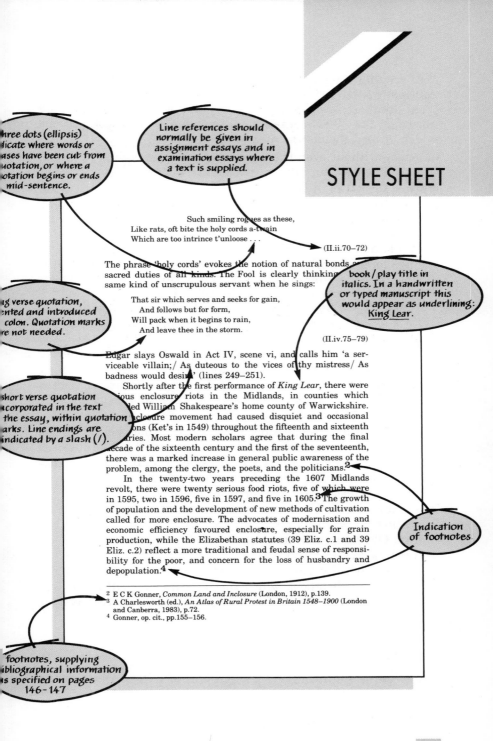

STYLE SHEET

three dots (ellipsis) indicate where words or phrases have been cut from quotation, or where a quotation begins or ends mid-sentence.

Line references should normally be given in assignment essays and in examination essays where a text is supplied.

Such smiling rogues as these,
Like rats, oft bite the holy cords a-twain
Which are too intrince t'unloose . . .

(II.ii.70–72)

The phrase 'holy cords' evokes the notion of natural bonds and sacred duties of all kinds. The Fool is clearly thinking same kind of unscrupulous servant when he sings:

book/play title in italics. In a handwritten or typed manuscript this would appear as underlining: <u>King Lear</u>.

long verse quotation, indented and introduced colon. Quotation marks are not needed.

That sir which serves and seeks for gain,
    And follows but for form,
Will pack when it begins to rain,
    And leave thee in the storm.

(II.iv.75–79)

short verse quotation incorporated in the text the essay, within quotation marks. Line endings are indicated by a slash (/).

Edgar slays Oswald in Act IV, scene vi, and calls him 'a serviceable villain;/ As duteous to the vices of thy mistress/ As badness would desire' (lines 249–251).

Shortly after the first performance of *King Lear*, there were ious enclosure riots in the Midlands, in counties which led William Shakespeare's home county of Warwickshire. enclosure movement had caused disquiet and occasional ons (Ket's in 1549) throughout the fifteenth and sixteenth ries. Most modern scholars agree that during the final ecade of the sixteenth century and the first of the seventeenth, there was a marked increase in general public awareness of the problem, among the clergy, the poets, and the politicians.[2]

In the twenty-two years preceding the 1607 Midlands revolt, there were twenty serious food riots, five of which were in 1595, two in 1596, five in 1597, and five in 1605.[3] The growth of population and the development of new methods of cultivation called for more enclosure. The advocates of modernisation and economic efficiency favoured enclosure, especially for grain production, while the Elizabethan statutes (39 Eliz. c.1 and 39 Eliz. c.2) reflect a more traditional and feudal sense of responsibility for the poor, and concern for the loss of husbandry and depopulation.[4]

Indication of footnotes

2 E C K Gonner, *Common Land and Inclosure* (London, 1912), p.139.
3 A Charlesworth (ed.), *An Atlas of Rural Protest in Britain 1548–1900* (London and Canberra, 1983), p.72.
4 Gonner, op. cit., pp.155–156.

footnotes, supplying bibliographical information specified on pages 146–147

143

We have divided the following information into two sections. Part A describes those rules which it is essential to master no matter what kind of essay you are writing (including examination answers). Part B sets out some of the more detailed conventions which govern the documentation of essays.

PART A: LAYOUT

Titles of texts

Titles of published books, plays (of any length), long poems, pamphlets and periodicals (including newspapers and magazines), works of classical literature, and films should be underlined: e.g. <u>David Copperfield</u> (novel), <u>Twelfth Night</u> (play), <u>Paradise Lost</u> (long poem), <u>Critical Quarterly</u> (periodical), Horace's <u>Ars Poetica</u> (Classical work), <u>Apocalypse Now</u> (film).

Notice how important it is to distinguish between titles and other names. <u>Hamlet</u> is the play; Hamlet the prince. <u>Wuthering Heights</u> is the novel; Wuthering Heights the house. Underlining is the equivalent in handwritten or typed manuscripts of printed italics. So what normally appears in this volume as *Othello* would be written as <u>Othello</u> in your essay.

Titles of articles, essays, short stories, short poems, songs, chapters of books, speeches, and newspaper articles are enclosed in quotation marks; e.g. 'The Flea' (short poem), 'The Prussian Officer' (short story), 'Middleton's Chess Strategies' (article), 'Thatcher Defects!' (newspaper headline).

Exceptions: Underlining titles or placing them within quotation marks does not apply to sacred writings (e.g. Bible, Koran, Old Testament, Gospels) or parts of a book (e.g. Preface, Introduction, Appendix).

It is generally incorrect to place quotation marks around a title of a published book which you have underlined. The exception is 'titles within titles': e.g. '<u>Vanity Fair</u>': A Critical Study (title of a book about *Vanity Fair*).

Quotations

Short verse quotations of a single line or part of a line should be incorporated within quotation marks as part of the running text of your essay. Quotations of two or three lines of verse are treated in the same way, with line endings indicated by a slash(/). For example:

1   In Julius Caesar, Antony says of Brutus, 'This was the noblest Roman of them all'.
2   The opening of Antony's famous funeral oration, 'Friends, Romans, Countrymen, lend me your ears;/ I come to bury Caesar not to praise him', is a carefully controlled piece of rhetoric.

Longer verse quotations of more than three lines should be indented from the main body of the text and introduced in most cases with a colon. Do not enclose indented quotations within quotation marks. For example:

It is worth pausing to consider the reasons Brutus gives to justify his decision to assassinate Caesar:

> It must be by his death; and for my part,
> I know no personal cause to spurn at him,
> But for the general. He would be crowned.
> How might that change his nature, there's the question.

At first glance his rationale may appear logical . . .

Prose quotations of less than three lines should be incorporated in the text of the essay, within quotation marks. Longer prose quotations should be indented and the quotation marks omitted. For example:

1   Before his downfall, Caesar rules with an iron hand. His political opponents, the Tribunes Marullus and Flavius, are 'put to silence' for the trivial offence of 'pulling scarfs off Caesar's image'.
2   It is interesting to note the rhetorical structure of Brutus's Forum speech:

> Romans, countrymen, and lovers, hear me for my cause, and be silent that you may hear. Believe me for my honour, and have respect to mine honour that you may believe. Censure me in your wisdom, and awake your senses, that you may the better judge.

Tenses: When you are relating the events that occur within a work of fiction, or describing the author's technique, it is the convention to use the present tense. Even though Orwell published *Animal Farm* in 1945, the book *describes* the animals' seizure of Manor Farm. Similarly, Macbeth always *murders* Duncan, despite the passage of time.

PART B: DOCUMENTATION

When quoting from verse of more than twenty lines, provide line references: e.g. In 'Upon Appleton House' Marvell's mower moves 'With whistling scythe and elbow strong' (l.393).

Quotations from plays should be identified by act, scene and line references: e.g. Prospero, in Shakespeare's The Tempest, refers to Caliban as 'A devil, a born devil' (IV.1.188). (i.e. Act 4. Scene 1. Line 188).

Quotations from prose works should provide a chapter reference and, where appropriate, a page reference.

Bibliographies should list full details of all sources consulted. The way is which they are presented varies, but one standard format is as follows:

1 Books and articles are listed in alphabetical order by the author's last name. Initials are placed after the surname.
2 If you are referring to a chapter or article within a larger work, you list it by reference to the author of the article or chapter, not the editor (although the editor is also named in the reference).
3 Give (in parentheses) the place and date of publication, e.g. (London, 1962). These details can be found within the book itself. Here are some examples:

> Brockbank, J. P., 'Shakespeare's Histories, English and Roman', in Ricks, C (ed.) English Drama to 1710 (Sphere History of Literature in the English Language) (London, 1971).
>
> Gurr, A., 'Richard III and the Democratic Process', Essays in Criticism 24 (1974), pp. 39–47.
>
> Spivack, B., Shakespeare and the Allegory of Evil (New York, 1958).

Footnotes: In general, try to avoid using footnotes and build your references into the body of the essay wherever possible. When you do use them give the full bibliographic reference to a work in the first instance and then use a short title: e.g. See K. Smidt, <u>Unconformities in Shakespeare's History Plays</u> (London, 1982), pp. 43–47 becomes Smidt (pp. 43–47) thereafter. Do not use terms such as 'ibid.' or 'op. cit.' unless you are absolutely sure of their meaning.

There is a principle behind all this seeming pedantry. The reader ought to be able to find and check your references and quotations as quickly and easily as possible. Give additional information, such as canto or volume number whenever you think it will assist your reader.

SUGGESTIONS FOR FURTHER READING

Texts

The following editions offer particularly stimulating Introductions:

Hunter, G K (ed.), *King Lear* (New Penguin Shakespeare; Harmondsworth, 1972)

Muir, K (ed.), *King Lear* (new Arden Shakespeare; London, 1952)

Wells, Stanley and Taylor, Gary, *The Complete Works* (The Oxford Shakespeare; Oxford, 1986)

Textual Studies

Taylor, G and Warren, M, *The Division of the Kingdom* (London, 1983)

Urkowitz, S, *Shakespeare's Revision of 'King Lear'* (London, 1985)

General studies (containing substantial discussions of *King Lear*)

Barton, A, 'Shakespeare: His Tragedies', in C Ricks (ed.), *English Drama to 1710* (Sphere History of Literature in the English Language; London, 1971)

Bradley, A C, *Shakespearean Tragedy* (London, 1904)

Dollimore, J, *Radical Tragedy* (Brighton, 1984)

Empson, W, *The Structure of Complex Words* (London, 1951)

Lerner, L D (ed.), *Shakespeare's Tragedies*, (Harmondsworth, 1963)

Wells, S (ed.), *The Cambridge Companion To Shakespeare* (Cambridge, 1986)

Studies of *King Lear*

Kermode, F (ed.), *King Lear* (Macmillan Casebooks; London, 1969)

Kozintsev, G, *King Lear: The Space of Tragedy* (London, 1977)

Mack, M, *King Lear in our Time* (Berkeley, California, 1965)

Muir, K, *King Lear* (Penguin Masterstudy series; Harmondsworth, 1986)

Muir, K and Wells, S (eds), *Aspects of King Lear* (Cambridge, 1982)

Orwell, G, 'Lear, Tolstoy and the Fool', in *Collected Essays and Journalism,* vol.4 (Harmondsworth, 1970)

Longman Group UK Limited
*Longman House, Burnt Mill, Harlow, Essex, CM20 2JE, England
and Associated Companies throughout the World.*

© Longman Group UK Limited 1988

First Published 1988
ISBN 0 582 00649 X

*Set in 10/12 pt Century Schoolbook, Linotron 202
Printed in Great Britain by Bell and Bain Ltd., Glasgow*

Acknowledgement
The editors would like to thank Zachary Leader for his assist-
ance with the style sheet.